PRAISE FOR *THE BUDDHA AND THE BEE*

"Life is an adventure. Cory Mortensen has captured the fun, wisdom, and sense of accomplishment gained from keeping your heart and mind open to life's gifts."

—Rob Angel, Creator of *Pictionary*
WSJ Bestsell~~~ ^ ~'

"This book gave me the refreshment I n
ly, it was a short vacation from everything t
While reading this memoir, I went through   p~~~~~~~
with the author and lived the lives and places I have no connections with. It triggered some suppressed desires that I'd buried deep down in my mind and compelled those emotions that were just too surreal."

—The Lectorem & Books

"At times, *The Buddha and the Bee* feels like what would happen if Jeff Spicoli, Sean Penn's iconic anti-hero from *Fast Times at Ridgemont High* had taken up biking and set his sights on San Francisco. Dude.

"*The Buddha and the Bee* sort of turns the idea of the inspirational memoir upside down, a few obscenities here and there joined at the hip by an occasional joint and near daily rural roadside Chinese dinners and overnight stays in forgotten America's roadside motels."

—Devon Street Review

"The only thing I didn't like about this book was that it ended. It's not just for bikers. It speaks to the heart of anyone who's ever wondered if their life is going in the right direction. Every page is a reminder that life is meant to be lived, not spent wishing for something to change. At best, this book will change your life. At worst, you'll be left hoping Saturn returns for you."

—Lisa T.

"Humorously written book that proves life isn't about the destination, but about the journey and all the beauty that unfolds if you simply allow life to come to you... with some effort of course.

"This book is a page turner. I found myself lying in bed at night laughing aloud at the situations the author experienced, while biking across the country. And at the same time, distilling life lessons that we all encounter into compassionate and simple statements that reminds us that we're all human, living life and wanting to be happy and smile... even when hardships come our way."

—F. Schilling

"Cory takes the reader on a journey into the vast landscapes of the American West and into his deepest thoughts. Told from an honest, emotional, funny, self-depreciating perspective, it gives the reader pause to reflect on their own life and perhaps light a fire or at least stir some dormant embers of a quest for adventure. If you are a fan of *Blue Highways, Fear and Loathing in Las Vegas, On the Road, Into the Wild, A Walk In the Woods* or other similar tome, then you should put *The Buddha and the Bee* on your reading list."

—John H.

"This guy is crazy, someone who you don't want planning a trip for you, but who you'd probably love to have beers with or read a book by. A great storyteller with tons of asides and background info. If you have any interest in biking cross country, reading this will either convince yourself to do it or never try such a thing. Hopefully if you decide to, you'll plan it out better than he did."

—E.W. Bertram

"I was in just the right mood to read a book like this. Different from my usual fiction, mysteries, etc, *The Buddha and the Bee* is the story of Cory Mortensen, who decides to make his way by bicycle from Minnesota to California with almost no supplies, no helmet, and practically no plan. Along the way, he meets his share of characters, eats a ton of Subway Italian sandwiches and Chinese food, stays in some of the country's sleaziest motels and takes in the sights in every town he visits—like the giant stuffed polar bear—The White King in Elko, Nevada. His bike breaks down multiple times, but he finally makes it to California.

"Cory Mortensen is a true free spirit. I have never done anything like he's done and I am envious. I hope he continues to have adventures and write about them! This book was a great change of pace for me from my normal reads and I enjoyed it immensely."

—Eileen

"This book is engaging, humorous, and a great escape during a pandemic. Interesting facts and trivia about the landscape and cities Mortensen travels through are an added bonus. This book is a gift to the reader to examine our own lives and reveal our adventurous spirit!"

— Joyce E.

"Cory Mortensen writes about his journey biking from Minnesota to California. I 'oh, no'ed' every time a car pulled up. And, I had a mini-anxiety response every time he blew out a tyre! What really caught my attention were the historical aspects of the towns he went through. Interesting, engaging, entertaining! Well written and witty."

—Angie

BOOKS BY CORY MORTENSEN

The Buddha and the Bee:
Biking through America's Forgotten Roadways
on an Accidental Journey of Discovery

Unlost:
Roaming through South America on a Spontaneous Journey

UNLOST

ROAMING THROUGH SOUTH AMERICA
ON A SPONTANEOUS JOURNEY

CORY MORTENSEN

Published by White Condor LLC

www.White-Condor.com

Hardcover: 978-1-7354981-8-8
Paperback: 978-1-7354981-6-4
Kindle: 978-1-7354981-9-5
EPUB: 978-1-7354981-0-2

Library of Congress Control Number: 2021918449

Publishing and Production by Concierge Marketing Inc.

Printed in the United States of America

10 9 8 7 6 5 4 3 2

This book is dedicated to the rucksack revolutionaries.

"I SEE A VISION OF A GREAT RUCKSACK REVOLUTION
THOUSANDS OR EVEN MILLIONS OF YOUNG AMERICANS
WANDERING AROUND WITH RUCKSACKS, GOING UP TO
MOUNTAINS TO PRAY, MAKING CHILDREN LAUGH AND
OLD MEN GLAD, MAKING YOUNG GIRLS HAPPY AND
OLD GIRLS HAPPIER, ALL OF 'EM ZEN LUNATICS WHO
GO ABOUT WRITING POEMS THAT HAPPEN TO APPEAR
IN THEIR HEADS FOR NO REASON AND ALSO BY BEING
KIND AND ALSO BY STRANGE UNEXPECTED ACTS KEEP
GIVING VISIONS OF ETERNAL FREEDOM TO EVERYBODY
AND TO ALL LIVING CREATURES."

– Jack Kerouac

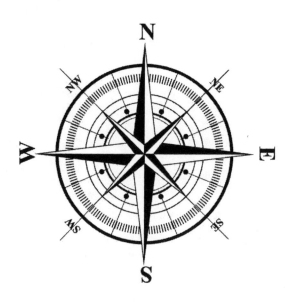

AUTHOR'S NOTE

This story starts where *The Buddha and the Bee* ends: the side of the Pacific Coast Highway across from Nepenthe in Big Sur, California, in October 2001.

While it's not necessary to read *The Buddha and the Bee* to enjoy this journey, there will be references to *The Buddha and the Bee* throughout, footnoted as TBATB.

If you have not already, I might suggest you put the brakes on this book, log on to your Amazon account, and start there. You can also go to www.TheBuddhaAndTheBee.com.

What you are about to read is based on actual occurrences. The dates, route, meals, and consumption are all true.

I have changed the names of those I actually know to avoid having to share any of the profits I make from this book with them. I have made up names for those I don't know or whose names I don't remember.

I HOPE THIS BOOK GUIDES IN SOME WAY
BUT THIS IS NOT A GUIDEBOOK

CONTENTS

PART 1:

I DIDN'T KNOW WHERE I WAS GOING EXACTLY, BUT I KNEW I WAS ON MY WAY.

PART 2
THE SAGA CONTINUES

PART 1:

I DIDN'T KNOW WHERE I WAS GOING EXACTLY, BUT I KNEW I WAS ON MY WAY.

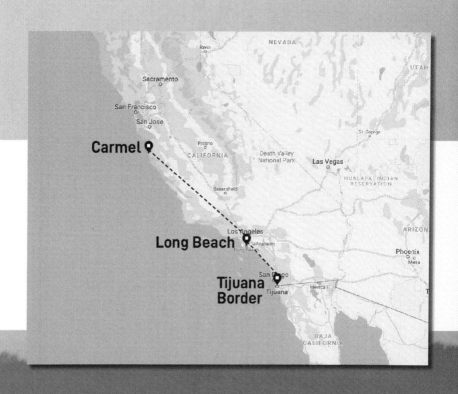

OCTOBER 29, 2001
California
Mexican Border

OCTOBER 29, 2001

Recently evicted at gun point, Gen and David didn't seem all that bothered by the fact that they no longer had a place to live. For them it was the open road. The freedom of working to live not living to work.

Their support group was an eccentric, childless aunt in San Diego who always kept her door open for them. And then there was the Rainbow Family—an international community claiming to be the "largest non-organization of non-members in the world." Their goal is to achieve peace and love on Earth.

For a couple of modern-day hippies, you wouldn't think a gas guzzling 1980s Jeep Cherokee would be their choice of transportation. When it comes to such free-spirited people living in a vehicle, we of course default to the Volkswagen Bus[1]—the symbol of freedom and anti-establishment. The ultimate counterculture mobile. When Jerry Garcia died, Volkswagen ran an ad of a VW Bus with a tear drop.

A pot smoking friend of mine had a Chrysler Caravan. That was his "hippy mobile."

"Cops aren't looking for a Chrysler Caravan," he told me as he passed the bong back to us on a road-trip to the hot springs in Ouray, Colorado, in 1995.

---

1 The people's car.

Gen and David's truck was jam-packed, complete with a rolled-up queen-size futon mattress and a very mellow dog, probably stoned from the heavy cloud of dope that hung in the air.

David was a genuinely nice guy who smiled a lot and appreciated the small stuff. Butterflies were of great interest to him. He was a carpenter, not licensed, mind you, that would be selling out. He had his own tools and was willing to work anywhere. I gave him the business card of the fight club guy I met in Hot Sulfur Springs who was looking for framers in Colorado.[2]

Gen was a know-it-all who would argue with you about your own experiences and tell you they didn't happen.

For example, in the case of how I ended up in the backseat of their truck, she matter-of-factly told me I had not biked from Minneapolis to California because "there isn't a bike trail that goes that far."[3]

I sat petting the dog that was now sleeping on my lap and watched the waves crash along the shore. Heading south along the California coast, I decided to stop in Long Beach, California, to see my uncle Charlie and aunt Diane.

Sea lions bathed on the coast near Gorda, California, and the occasional dolphin appeared in the surf. I hoped to see a whale but no such luck.

The air was fresh. A cool wind off the ocean cleansed the Jeep of the lingering reefer smell as we rode with the windows down after leaving San Simeon, California.

2 TBATB
3 TBATB

I was second guessing my early retirement. What did I do? Why did I give up a great job? A successful career? Maybe I could call Mark back and get my job back.[4] It had only been a day or two since I resigned. For the first time since I had a paper route, I was unemployed.

In Santa Barbara, we grabbed some food from a taco truck. A flyer on a post advertised that the Dead Kennedys were performing in a couple days. I was a big fan of punk in the eighties. The Dead Kennedys were a favorite, but without Jello Biafra, eh, they just weren't the Dead Kennedys.

Gen and David dropped me off in Long Beach, where I spent two nights at Charlie and Diane's. Charlie and I went out for a run and discussed important and non-important things. For ten years, he had tried to convince me to move out to California, pointing out the fact that there were a lot of single beautiful women. I should have settled right then and there, but something was pulling me to continue south.

A Greyhound to México was six and a half hours. The guy next to me was a large fella named James.

He was a retired bus driver on his way to see his son who was a Marine at Camp Pendleton.

James decided, for whatever reason, to tell me the following story. A story he claimed to have never told anyone else. I was intrigued.

4 TBATB

I was taking a group of people on a tour around the United States. The route took the tour through Chicago. I recall arriving around 9:00 p.m.

After dropping off the passengers at the front door of the hotel, there was a place around back designated for buses to park. Backing up the bus, the back of the bus hung over into another vacant lot.

While sitting in the bus completing my paperwork, I heard a woman scream in the back of the bus.

Looking back, I saw just an empty bus and chalked it up to an overactive imagination and continued with my paperwork.

I heard another scream, and in the bus mirror, I saw a woman pop her head up over one of the back seats and then duck down.

I went back to investigate, checking every row. I found nothing.

As I headed back toward the front of the bus, I heard a woman scream again. It came from underneath me. Armed with a crowbar, I exited the bus and opened all the underneath storage compartments. As I opened each door, they revealed nothing. I then walked around the bus, went back inside, grabbed my paperwork, and left immediately to go back to the hotel.

The staff noticed I was a little shaken up and asked what happened. I told them the story.

They told me that the vacant lot, which the back end of the bus hung over, was once an abandoned building where many women had been raped and killed and many people had claimed to hear a woman screaming.

James got off the bus in Oceanside, California.

I liked his story; I like ghost stories. I believe in ghosts and aliens and the supernatural. Some things can't be explained by science. Perhaps one day a new dimension will expose itself to all of us, and it will be amazing. A supernatural celebration of beings from other realms, universes, and afterworlds. MC'd by Vincent Price. Might be a good time.

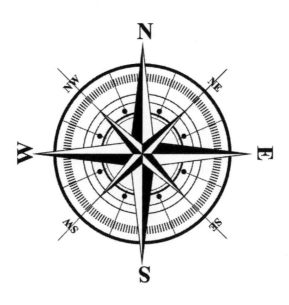

MEXICAN BORDER

After the recent events of September 11, I thought the border crossing was going to be a great big ordeal, complete with a heavy police or military presence.

I envisioned a dystopian gauntlet of soldiers lined up in full body armor, faces hidden behind reflecting helmets, machine guns pressed diagonally across their chests. Large, empty, organized, emotionless, and intimidating.

A long row of fascist-styled flags with some sort of black authoritarian symbol prominently centered in a sea of red, letting you know the presence of a powerful, faceless government was in control.

Black helicopters scoured the sky on both sides of the line.

Troops running alongside tanks, rushing to a recent explosion. A bomb set off by an insurgent group or perhaps a false alarm, an overworked transformer reminding us of our fragile power grid.

Over the loudspeaker, a familiar comforting female voice echoing Orwellian platitudes in English and Spanish.

War is Peace – La guerra es paz

Slavery is Freedom – La esclavitud es libertad

Ignorance is Strength – Ignorancia es fuerza

Instead, I stood in a rather fast-moving line of Mexicans carrying goods back from their day of shopping at the Las Americas Premium Outlets.

When I approached, with passport open, the disinterested immigration officer just waved me through. He didn't even look at my passport, much less stamp it.

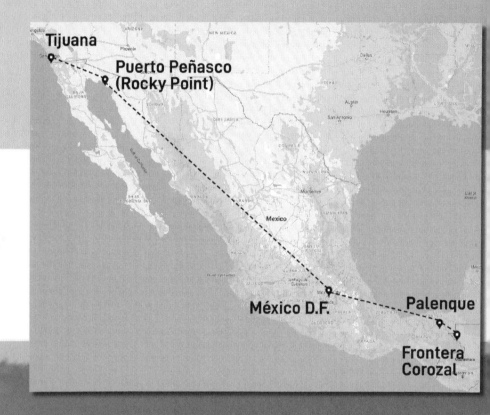

MÉXICO
Puerto Peñasco (Rocky Point)
México D.F.
Palenque

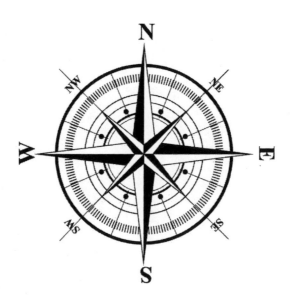

MÉXICO

"Land of the War God"

My past experience arriving in México via airplane was that immigration had always been a tad more serious.

A green-and-red-light system "randomly" decided if you were selected for a more involved inspection by the traveler pressing a button, any confusion easily resolved with a bribe. The system later evolved into an automated system. Bribes went down.

Once, flying into México, I got picked. The officer handed me my passport and pointed to a quiet corner. "When you come back, there will be something for me in this passport."

I returned and handed him my passport. Opening it, he was less than impressed with my offering. "Hey, all I have is that five."

Entering México via the land border apparently immigration officers took a bit more of a relaxed approach.

A couple of years prior, I had flown to Belize for ten days. I'd do some diving off Caye Caulker and then explore a bit of the country. I met a guy in Punta Gorda who offered to take me in his small fishing boat to Livingston, Guatemala—a small fishing village.

From there, I took a "chicken" bus up to Flores, visited Tikal and then returned to Belize to fly home.

Problem was, I didn't get a stamp out of Belize or into Guatemala, so when I arrived at the border to leave Guatemala, it didn't even cross my mind there would be an issue.

The Guatemalan immigration officer was not as flexible. He went through my passport four or five times and asked where my stamp was entering Guatemala.

"I don't have one. I took a boat to Guatemala from Belize, and there was no immigration control." There was, but I didn't know about it, ask about it, or seek it out. Instead, I drank beers with a local fisherman and caught a bus north.

"Seventy dollars."

"Seventy dollars for what?"

"It will cost you seventy dollars to get a stamp to exit."

"I'm not going to pay seventy dollars. I don't even have seventy dollars."

"You must pay!"

"I'll just go to Belize and try my luck. After all, according to my passport, I'm not even here."

He didn't like that response and took my passport, placing it on the desk, then directed the next in line to approach him and hand over their passport. While he was busy shuffling through their passport, I reached over and took mine back, walked out, and headed over to the Belize immigration.

"Where is your Guatemala exit stamp?" the officer asked as he shuffled through my passport.

"I don't have one. They wanted seventy dollars."

"Seventy dollars!? Ha ha." He shook his head, and a second Belize entry was placed into my passport.

Belize and Guatemala were still in the midst of a land dispute that went back to the seventeenth century. For the most part, Guatemalans didn't recognize Belize as an independent country.

Spain claimed all of Central America as theirs. However, there was already a colony of British slave owners, who Spain considered outlaws, who settled into what was known as British Honduras. In 1973, British Honduras became Belize, a commonwealth of Britain and the only Latin American country where English is the official language. God save the Queen.

In 2008, the dispute between Guatemala and Belize was finally resolved.

With this stamp-less passport episode bouncing around in my head, my goal was to find an immigration office that would stamp my passport, proving I legally entered México on the off chance I might exit México on the south border where immigration might or might not be more strict.

The immigration office was surprisingly unassuming and out of the way, considering the San Ysidro border was the busiest US–México border crossing between the two countries with thirty-six million people crossing every year. You would think there would be some sort of impressive government building, with a lobby, counters with bulletproof glass, signs in various languages placed predominately on walls as you entered, and an oversized Mexican flag hanging from exposed steel rafters. Wanted posters and travel brochures, crying children and flustered parents.

Instead, it was a lonely guy in a military-style uniform, sitting at an old steel desk wedged in a dead-end hallway.

I handed him my passport, and he looked at me as if to say, "Why are you handing me your passport?"

"¿Habla English?"

"Yes, I speak English."

"Could I please have you stamp my passport?"

He looked at my passport and then at me and gave a little scoff. Handing it back, he said, "You don't need a stamp."

It was true, I didn't need a stamp. In 2001, I really didn't even need a passport to be in México as a US citizen, but I thought it wise to avoid the whole Guatemala-Belize incident.

Guatemala, if I kept going south, would be my next border crossing.

"I am going to be leaving México in the south."

He stared at me while he opened the top drawer of his desk. He pulled out the stamp, pounded the imprint on my passport, and with a tinge of sarcasm said, "De nada."

"Gracias," I replied, grabbing my passport.

"If you go more than one hundred kilometers into México, you must pay a twenty-five-dollar tax. You must pay at bank. There is one across the street." Handing me a form, he smiled, knowing the whole thing was bullshit.

It was bullshit, and I dealt with the form the same way I dealt with parking tickets. I threw it away.

Leaving at six p.m., it was a seven-hour bus ride to Puerto Peñasco, aka Rocky Point. A quick weekend getaway to the beach for Arizonians.

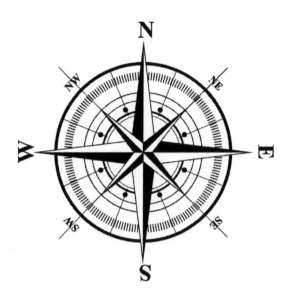

PUERTO PEÑASCO (ROCKY POINT)

B y the time I exited the bus and found Playa Hermosa Beach, it was about one thirty in the morning. Not having a watch, I was totally guessing. The beach was dark and empty. I could see the whitecaps and foam of the water as it reached the shore and scurried back into the dark sea.

Lights from the town offered a nice hue to sleep under as I pulled out my sleeping bag and crawled in for the night, the Sea of Cortés just twenty feet away.

One or two hours into my slumber, a bright light suddenly woke me up. I could barely make out the silhouettes of two people. I was comforted knowing it wasn't the three little aliens I ran into back in Utah.[5]

In fact, it was two police officers. They started yelling at me in Spanish. I didn't understand what they were saying. It was dark, a bright light was in my eye, and I was still trying to wake up and process the situation. There was only one thing I could think to do and that was to roll over and ignore them.

They moved around me and shined the light again in my face, shouting at me and pointing toward town. I rolled over again.

This continued for about two minutes until the light was shut off and they walked away.

I had heard somewhere that beaches in México were public— not sure how true that was.

I also heard somewhere that Mexican jails were not as nice as the cold, gray concrete cells we have in the United States, possibly speaking from experience.

About thirty people were on the beach when the sun rose. I climbed out of my bag, stripped down to my shorts, and took a bath in the sea.

The water was cold and refreshing. I bobbed with the waves; the undertow pulled me further from the shore. The sea was in control now. Laying back, water clapped into my ears. I licked the salt from my lips. Eyes closed, I was weightless and wondered what was next.

1.   Go home – No, not yet.
2.   Head south – Most probably, but where and for what point?
3.   Find a job here in Puerto Peñasco – A bartender or a tour guide. Find myself a nice Mexican girl, her father a farmer, her mother known for her homemade tortillas, which she sold in the market. We'd buy several small properties and rent them out to gringos. Our small family would soon grow and my visits back to the United States would be less and less frequent. I would perhaps take up fishing and never fully grasp the Spanish language.

Swimming back to the shore, I packed up my sleeping bag. It was early, dogs scavenged, roosters crowed, kids in uniforms hung out before school, loitering in the streets. I was hungry and went on the hunt for huevos con arroz y frijoles.

In hindsight I should have stopped along the way. Maybe got off in Guaymas, done some hiking in Nacapule Canyon, or summit Mount Tetakawi. Instead, I bought a bus ticket for a forty-hour journey to México D.F.[6]

What was forty hours on a bus like?

It started with pleasantries with your new neighbor, perhaps helping them with their overhead luggage. You might have several neighbors along a forty-hour journey, people entering and exiting at each stop. Edward Hall's concept of "personal space" didn't exist here.

Once seated and settled, that was when the fight for the arm rest began. No talking was involved here, more of an elbow version of thumb war, duked out as passive aggressively as possible. The first sign of weakness and you'd have lost territory. Then you plotted your attack, carefully watching out of the corner of your eye for your enemy's weakness and then you struck again.

My must-haves for long distance bus rides include, but are not limited to, the following:

- Blanket or sleeping bag: Bring it. The temperature will hover around thirty-five degrees for hours at a time, then the temperature will shoot up to eighty or ninety degrees and then back down to thirty-five.

- Ear plugs: In case you want to tune out the poorly dubbed action movies that play at very loud volumes.

---

6 México Distrito Federal (D.F.) was officially renamed Ciudad de México in 2016.

- Book(s): Better have one or two.

- CD Player and CDs: Remember this was 2001, so we didn't have iThings. But for those of you who don't have a portable CD player, bring your iThing.

- Food: Load up on snacks but never turn down the vendors or local restaurants when the bus stops.

- Adult Beverage(s): It just so happens, by some sort of miracle of modern-day science, that the contents in a bottle of wine fits nicely into a Nalgene bottle.

Why should I complain about arm rests and fifty-degree temperature swings? I was on my way to do what I had been telling myself I wanted to do—see the world.

Travel isn't always sexy; it's hard and complicated. Frustrating and frighting. You are in foreign lands, your family really has no idea where you are, half the time you don't really even know where you are. Language skills may be limited to only: Hello, thank you, and how much is this? You're now the minority, stared at, targeted, harassed in some cases for being different.

Things don't always happen as planned, and sometimes there are no plans and things just happen. Amazing things, adventures you would never experience at home. New smells, new foods, new people, narrow escapes.

It was time I owned up to all the talking I had done about how I was going to see the world. It was my time to go deeper into myself. I had shed so much personal baggage on the bike ride,[7] this was a different concept entirely. I just jumped off into the deep end

---

7 TBATB

and would learn that it was even deeper than I thought and would continue to get deeper and deeper.

I was in a different land. I didn't understand the conversations around me. I wasn't on my bike. I gave up a small bit of control to a bus driver who I didn't know and could only hope had years of experience and no accidents.

I thought about a poem by Guillaume Apollinaire, which I included in my high school graduation speech.

> "Come to the edge," he said.
> "We can't, we're afraid!" they responded.
> "Come to the edge," he said.
> "We can't, we will fall!" they responded.
> "Come to the edge," he said.
> And so they came.
> And he pushed them.
> And they flew.

I said these words as a challenge to my classmates, those in the audience who were actually paying attention, and as a personal promise to myself that I would fly.

There were no more excuses. It was time to fly.

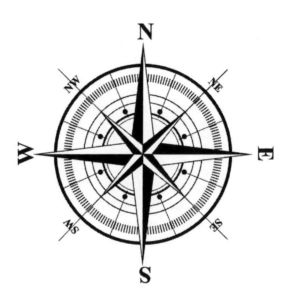

MÉXICO D.F.

O nce in México D.F., I took a taxi to Hostel Mundo Joven Catedral, in the historic center of the city just one block off Plaza del Zócalo.

Taxis in México D.F. were predominately old VW Bugs sans a front passenger seat. While the lack of the front seat made it easier for a passenger to get in the back, at first glance, I was reminded of the serial killer Ted Bundy, who infamously removed the passenger seat in his 1968 VW Bug so he could lay his victims flat to hide them.

It was about midafternoon, and I was ready for a cocktail. It just so happened on the rooftop of the hostel was a bar-restaurant that overlooked the back façade of Catedral Metropolitana de la Ciudad de México.

It was the first time I was in with my new tribe. They didn't know me, I didn't know them, but we all shared a common idea…a philosophy. Perhaps a pilgrimage, a reinvention, or reacquaintance of oneself. Out here we could each be whoever we wanted to be, or didn't want to be. International prejudices in this community seemed not to exist. Backpackers were one of the many magical aspects of travel.

Backpackers are an international collage of experiences, personalities, and emotions. We come in all shapes, colors, and ages.

An experiment really, of what a truly borderless world could look like. A different kind of Rainbow Family, a massive group of disorganized members belonging to the same ideology.

Citizens of the world: Flags mean everything to some and nothing to others.

In 1953 Garry Davis created the "World Government of World Citizens." Complete with passport. Giving a person "the political representation of a sovereign citizen of the world dynamically, intrinsically allied with sovereign humanity."

The idea was that a world citizen was not bound by any political rights and duties required from a country, but rather a world citizen was a human with their rights and duties within the world community itself. A philosophy I could solidly get behind.

Cover of the World Passport

We, in the USA, chant "USA" because we were born in the USA. But had one been born in Germany or Egypt or Kiribati, would they not chant for their country? The place they were born, with the same passion and intensity instilled in them from a sort of political and family "indoctrination"? Of course, we see this play out every four years during the opening ceremony of the Olympics.

Indoctrination. Perhaps that's the wrong word, or maybe it is the perfect word.

Why is my team better than your team? After all, my team and your team only exist because someone on another team drew lines on a map to indicate which team you are on. Some of us are born into a team that we like. Others choose to change teams later down the road after realizing that they want to be on a different team.

I have had the opportunity to meet many of these backpackers over my years of short-term travels, staying at hostels or pensions,[8] with all of their possessions fitting into a forty-liter backpack. They are some of the richest people in the world. Rich with experience.

The Swedish woman I met in Cancún and traveled to Cuba with[9] was getting away after the death of her grandmother, whom she was very close with.

A woman from Belgium, who I crossed paths with in Ecuador, learned her father was sexually abusing her sister for the past decade and decided to leave permanently, never to return. The backstories were often tough and impossible to relate to.

Two factory workers from the UK in their fifties had never left Bristol, England. One day they realized they had spent their entire

8   Guest house or boarding house.
9   TBATB

life in a factory. Unhappy, they sold everything to travel the world. I ran into them in a thatched hut in Costa Rica.

One of the more entertaining run-ins was in 1997, with a guy who referred to himself as "Dr. Love." The fiftyish-year-old black guy with five teeth was a former resident of San Quentin State Prison and "lived" in Central America during the winter only to return monthly to pick up a welfare check. I met him in El Salvador, and we traveled to Belize together. He dragged a suitcase with a broken handle and three working wheels. In the summer, he lived in Venice Beach, California, as a sort of fixture off the boardwalk, charging money in exchange for advice about, well, Love.

I ran into to Dr. Love again on the boardwalk in Venice Beach in 1999 after completing the Long Beach Marathon.

Then there were those just wanting to simply surf a new beach, search for enlightenment, practice yoga in the jungle. Ride their bike some great distance over personally uncharted lands. Sail the oceans. Others might come to volunteer and stay or come to travel and end up volunteering. Help build a school or teach English or make a community somehow better than it was. Brought this to mind:

> "NOT ALL THOSE WHO WANDER ARE LOST."
> — *J.R.R. Tolkien*

There are those who might fit into another box, if I were to create boxes. They traveled but in search of nothing—nothing they were yet aware of. They traveled because they could. Perhaps I might have fallen into that category, at least for now. Having sold my house and with over a decade of savings, I had years' worth of funding to wander and explore the world, or perhaps sit on a beach and learn to surf.

It's a timeless, dateless existence. No clock to punch, no day to be somewhere unless self-imposed. Perhaps a flight to here or a bus to there. One could read those books they have been putting off or write that novel. Create that piece of art or draw up a business plan.

This is another aspect that all backpackers share regardless of the reason for their individual journey.

I find one of the most overlooked quality of backpackers is their ability to problem solve. If I was a Human Resource director and had two candidates, one who had a four-year degree or one who had a one-year gap and only two years of university, I'd go with the gap year.

Every day you must deal with working out situations, currency exchange, budgeting, understanding laws of immigration, and adapting to new cultures. Always learning, always thinking, always adapting, and always problem-solving. Finding and negotiating services such as laundry, lodging, transportation in foreign lands, perhaps not knowing the language. You are often forced to make decisions that go against your original plans due to unforeseen circumstance. A train derails, a bus tips over, a war breaks out, a banking system collapses, a passport is stolen. Now what? You got to figure that shit out!

I had a purchased a round-trip ticket to Cuba from México back in the 1990s. My last night, I met a Czech woman, and we enjoyed a lot of music, dancing, and mojitos. Come sunrise, all I had left was a US twenty-dollar bill—I had only myself to blame for this.

It as one of the new twenties. So new, no taxi driver would take it as they thought it was counterfeit. The airport was not within walking distance. I was running out of time to catch my flight, which I had pre-paid for, and options were limited. I tried a few ATMs, but my debit card didn't work because of the embargo. I ended up negotiating really hard with one taxi driver who finally agreed to take my twenty in exchange for a ride to the airport.

Once at the airport, they asked for a thirty-dollar departure tax that I was told by the travel agent who sold me the ticket was included with my airfare. Humbly, I found myself panhandling for thirty dollars. An Iranian guy, who had defected to Canada in 1982 to avoid fighting in the Iran–Iraq war, gave me the money. "I didn't want to fight in a war to kill my cousins." I'd repay him in Cancún.

Being Middle Eastern, once we arrived in México, the police walked right up to him and detained him for no reason other than profiling. He was an engineer in Canada. Now he was thrown into a situation he had to work out.

The whole time I was trying to figure out how to get on that pre-paid flight, I was also thinking of other ways to get off this island and back to the United States. My only other option would be to find a harbor, look for sailboats from the USA, and hitch the ninety miles north.

You work it out, and I can assure you based on some people I know and have worked with, not very many people can make a Starbucks order decision much less negotiate a life-or-death situation in a foreign country under pressure. The fact is, once you are out there alone, you're just a person nobody knows and nobody cares about. There are kind people out there so pay that Karma forward, because out here, you're going to need it.

Over a beer, I met a couple of backpackers at the rooftop bar. The woman was a young braless blonde from Germany, who was apparently a bit chilly. She was in the process of convincing two Kiwi guys that the human body didn't need food or water to live.

The Kiwis had only been traveling for about two months, which sounds long by United States standards since we typically only get two weeks of vacation a year. They started in San Francisco and worked their way down hitchhiking, opting to spend time in Baja, California, learning to kiteboard.

Zee German had been out wandering for over five years, or so she told us with her British English accent, having learned English in London.

She believed in breatharianism, that sunlight was all one needed to survive. It was the main source vital for life. It wouldn't surprise you to know that many who truly believe in breatharianism die of starvation.

During our conversation, the waitress came over and our German friend ordered some chips and guacamole, which of course begged the question, "We thought you didn't need food to live?"

"I don't. I just like the taste of it."

My first full day in México D.F. started off wandering around a sort of made-up perimeter. First, a few blocks this way, then a couple that way, then which way and aft way. I loved the pedestrian dominance of the calles and avenidas. Mexican flags draped off second- and third-floor windows and police directed traffic along the perfectly constructed cobblestone streets.

I entered all the cathedrals I came across:

Name	Type	Built
Templo de San Felipe Neri or "La Profesa"	Baroque	1610
Nuestra Señora de Loreto Church	Baroque	1809
Templo de Santa Inés	Baroque	1790
Church of San Bernardo	Baroque	1685

Each with its heavy use of incense, which hung plentifully in the air. All full of grandeur and gold and art and rich woodwork and seemingly unlimited resources.

Each cathedral felt cold and hollow. Light danced around the nave and chancel, brought in from the abundance of stained glass. Jesus hung on a cross above the altar in the apse. Saints looked down in sorrow as the stations of the cross surrounded the sanctuary.

Shrouded old women prayed in pews and holy water at your service was available in the holy water font stationed at each entrance.

Meandering down a side street, I came across an old Mexican man dressed in a tweed hunting jacket. He sat at a small café table on the sidewalk with a young woman from Quebec. We engaged in some pleasantries, and the next thing I knew, they asked me to join them as they shared a bottle of wine.

We discussed the current state of affairs, focusing on the War on Terror. He had seen much in his years; she had seen less. I, perhaps, was somewhere in the middle and listened as they shared their thoughts on the matter in English. We ordered a second bottle.

If there was anyone who was going to save the planet it was Dominque from Quebec. The War on Terror was minor in the whole sphere of issues Mother Earth had on her plate. There were the rising coast lines, global droughts, starving polar bears…

Our second bottle consumed, we split la cuenta and went our separate ways.

The Catedral Metropolitana de la Ciudad de México (Gothic, 1813) overlooked Plaza del Zócalo, now known as Plaza de la Constitución.

Around 1325 AD, the Aztec city of Tenochtitlán was established. Next to the plaza was a sacred temple that was the absolute center of the city and the universe, according to the Aztec. The Spanish tore it all down, literally, and started work on the cathedral in 1573.

México D.F. was currently the oldest continuously inhabited capital city in the Americas.

And just in case you were interested: Argolis, Greece, was the oldest continuously inhabited city in the world, going back seven thousand years.

The next day, I graduated to jumping on the light rail and taking it to the end of the line—Tasqueña Station. From there, I explored the streets back to Plaza del Zócalo, seven miles north.

It was a really wonderful walk back. The city was lush and cleaner than expected, street artist graffiti left very few buildings alone.

Av. Plutarco had a fantastic green space that separated the avenue, two lanes on both sides, a third for parking. Exercise equipment, benches, food and beverage vendors, and playground swings catered to an upper middle class. Taxis laid in wait while old men read newspapers and fed birds.

México D.F. was the largest city in the world.[10] With that comes a sort of melting pot of people, so for the most part I blended in. The ethnicity breakdown of México D.F. is:

21% Indigenous Mexicans (Native American)

25% Mestizo (Indigenous + European)

47% Light-skinned Mexican or White Mexicans

1% Asian-Mexicans (mostly Asian or Asian descendent)

0.1% Afro-Mexicans (mostly Black or Black descendent)

1% Not classified

So being a tanned, white, blond guy walking around México D.F. meant I didn't really stick out as much as one might assume.

Thanks to a genetic mutation somewhere along the DNA line, only 2 percent of people in the world are natural blonds. In regards to México D.F., it so happens that 18 percent of the population has natural blond hair. That's on par for the United States, which comes in around 20 percent. Finland takes the lead at 58 percent.

10 In 2001, México City was the largest city in the world by population. In 2021, it was the fifth largest by population.

My last day in México D.F. I was a bit under the weather. Well, at least I thought I was getting sick. It turned out I was just dehydrated.

I started reading my newly acquired *Lonely Planet* about all the diseases I could contract in this neck of the woods.

Down the street was a farmacia. After reading about malaria and all the places it could be contracted, I decided to pick up some antimalarial pills and a few syringes in case I ever needed an inoculation. Rumor had it that new needles were not always used further south.

Rumor also had it that the invention of the gin and tonic was introduced by the British army. Tropical regions with malaria devastated the troops, so Dr. George Cleghorn mixed quinine with tonic and, to help soften the horrible taste, gin was added.

One would need to drink eighteen gallons of tonic to fend off malaria. The way I pour gin and tonics, that would also be eighteen gallons of gin.

The lady at the counter at the farmicia gave me a book listing thousands and thousands of medications and a prescription book. My instructions were to find the antimalarial pills I wanted, write my prescription, and then she would fill up a bottle for me.

Potential side effects of antimalarial pills are nausea, vomiting, vivid dreams, confusion, dizziness, and hallucinations.

My medicinal options were:

- Atovaquone/Proguanil
- Chloroquine
- Doxycycline
- Mefloquine
- Primaquine
- Tafenoquine

A pretty stress-free task (he says sarcastically) that took me close to forty minutes to complete, and in the end, I didn't know if the Chloroquine pills I chose would cause nausea or hallucinations. I was sort of hoping for the latter.

I took a taxi to the bus station and bought a ticket to Palenque. I had heard that Palenque was a must-see Mayan site.

Not learning anything from my forty-hour bus ride from Rocky Point, the twelve-hour bus ride should have been broken up with a stop in Coatzacoalcos, A coastal town that was home to the Olmec.

The Olmec were the first Mesoamerican people to understand things like the concept of "zero." They developed a writing system, calendar, farming, and some say—popcorn. Most notable were the giant Olmec heads they created, some as large as eleven feet high with African and Asian features, leading to speculation of some sort of trans-oceanic connection.

Example of an Olmec head (Stock Photo)

The names found in the Yucatán and Quintana Roo states sounded cool to the foreigner, but their English translations didn't exactly scream vacation location:

- Coatzacoalcos: Where the snake hides
- Cancún: Nest of snakes
- Cozumel: Island of swallows
- Tulum: Wall
- Campeche: Place of snakes and ticks
- Yucatán: While there are many stories as to the definition of the name, my favorite legend is the word Yucatán was the single response given by the Mayan to the Spanish when asked what the name of the region was called: I do not understand you.

On the bus, I met Paul, a Canadian who was just wrapping up his time as a university exchange student in México D.F.. I had a backpack; he had a suitcase with wheels. He was going to stop in Córdoba, but after hearing where I was going, he decided to modify his plans and join me in exploring Palenque.

From the bus terminal in Palenque, we asked the taxi to drop us off at the Jungle Palace Hostel. It was a rustic hodgepodge of concrete-supported thatched huts, partially overtaken by the jungle that surrounded them.

A dirt road cut through the jungle leading to the "office." A limited food menu and cold beers were available, and they had a shaman who was on call to guide you during your magic mushroom experience, if you so chose. Magic mushrooms were sold by the "magic mushroom guy" down the road.

That night we met two women from England, Robin and Nicki, at one of the outside tables, where a group of backpackers had gathered for food and drink.

Robin and Nicki were on a one-year journey. They shared with us that they had purchased an Around-the-World airplane ticket.

I had never heard of an Around-the-World ticket and was totally taken in by the brilliance of the idea. Apparently, you had one year to complete the trip and could only travel in one direction. Additionally, you could land in one city and get back on a flight from another city. Robin and Nicki had just landed in México D.F.. They planned to travel by land for a few months and pick up their next and final flight from Buenos Aires home to London.

When we met Robin and Nicki, they had just returned from Palenque and were headed to Tikal, Guatemala, next.

"Look, Paul and I are going to Palenque tomorrow. If you guys stick around another day, we would love to join you to Tikal."

"Yes, that sounds lovely," they both agreed.

We discussed their past travels and future destinations over many beers and then I proposed a grand idea.

"Guys, I met someone at a hostel in México D.F. who told me there is a crossing from México to Guatemala that is less traveled. I don't know how reliable the information is, but it sounds like it could be a little adventure. We find transportation from here to Frontera Corozal, which is about three hours away. From there, we find someone with a boat who will take us down a river to Bethel, Guatemala. It's about forty-five minutes. From there, we take a bus to Flores. What do you think?"

"Yes, that sounds amazing," Robin agreed.

PALENQUE

The ruins of Palenque were just a four kilometer walk from the hostel. Paul and I reached the entrance just after the site opened. We went our own ways. I preferred to be alone while exploring such locations as ruins.

I wandered around the Temple of the Inscriptions, rubbing the stones that were carved and brought here 1300 years earlier.

Palenque offered many structures to explore:

- Temple of the Count
- Palace of Palenque
- Temple of the Cross
- Temple XIII
- Temple of the Foliated Cross

Paul found me as I left the Temple of the Sun.

"Dude, follow me." Paul led me back to the main structure, The Palace.

"Cory, this is Roberto. He is part Mayan. His grandmother is Mayan, and he said there is a Mayan village we can hike to with him. What do you think?"

"I think we should do it."

What could go wrong, following a complete stranger to an unknown village somewhere in the jungles of México?

The trail led us straight through the jungle and started to climb over a mountain. I could see a silhouette of a toucan joined to tree branches as howler monkeys shook the tree canopy around us. It was darker in the jungle, not complete darkness but a mysterious sort of shadowless land that was cool with soft edges, strange sounds, and new smells.

Out of the jungle, we found ourselves on top of a high hill. Farmland for a local community, men with sticks tediously planted rice on steep, sloping hillsides. One small hole punched into the earth with a stick, seed inserted. Average annual income around here was eight thousand USD.

"Look down," Roberto said to us.

We looked down and seashells were scattered all around us.

Roberto scanned the area with his arm and said, "All of this was once underwater."

In fact, it was part of the Western Interior Seaway.[11] Reaching down, I grabbed a handful of small shells, each no bigger than a dime. It was quite fascinating to think, while standing at the top of this hill, that millions of years ago, plesiosaurs and mosasaurs swam above where we were standing. Fossils of fish, shark teeth, and sting-ray bones were commonly found throughout the area.

I wasn't entirely sure if the village we finally arrived at had a name. If it did have a name, Roberto didn't share it with us, nor did we ask.

Mysterious and exotic, the children ran toward Paul and me smiling and laughing. Each reaching out and touching our hairy

11 TBATB

arms. We were the "white gorillas," the first white people some of these kids had ever seen.

We arrived at Roberto's grandmother's house. She only spoke Mayan. Roberto also spoke Mayan along with Spanish, English, and a little German.

While Moses was bringing the Ten Commandments down from Mt. Sinai, and Hinduism was getting its legs in India, and the Shang Dynasty in China was developing a writing system, the Mayans were starting their civilization in the jungle of Belize. A civilization that would develop one of the most sophisticated systems of writing, art, astronomy, and architecture. Am I missing a few other achievements, like the creation of a calendar and creating crops? Yes, I am.

I had to admit I didn't even know Mayan was still spoken, but as it turned out, it is one of the oldest languages spoken in the world today by nearly six million people.

Tamil is the oldest language, spoken by seventy-seven million people, and one of the official languages of India, Singapore, and Sri Lanka.

Roberto and his grandmother conversed for a short time, while Paul and I played fútbol with the kids on the street. The kids were quick and agile with their makeshift ball of tape-wrapped garbage. We didn't stand a chance, they won four to nil.

Me, Roberto, and Roberto's Mayan grandmother

We made it back to the hostel just before dusk and worked out our game plan to cross over into Guatemala. There were not a lot of ways to get to Frontera Corozal. The person at the hostel arranged for transportation. While this was not a common border crossing, it was also not uncommon.

Waiting on the dirt road, a dog walked up to Paul's suitcase, lifted its leg, and pissed on it just as a white van was pulling up. I wasn't as leery about the white van as I was on my bike trip[12]. The transportation sat up to eight people. It was just the four of us, the driver, and two armed men with machine guns and bulletproof vests.

The rest of us had t-shirts and shorts except Paul, who was wearing jeans and a long sleeve shirt. We felt confident that if a firefight broke out the dudes with the bulletproof vests might survive to tell our kin what happened on that fateful day in November somewhere in the Mexican state of Chiapas.

12 TBATB

According to one of the armed men, there were drugs and gangs all around us. He lifted his machine gun and said, "But we are protected." His gold tooth shone as he smiled.

The road was narrow, paved, and lacked any semblance of a shoulder. Asphalt cut through the tall, broadleaf evergreen forest. We chased that vanishing point for almost three hours. It would have taken me two days if I were on my bike.

Frontera Corozal would be best described as a sleepy town, laid out like a perfect, unimaginative grid. Simple homes made of stucco and thatched roofs lined the town's dirt roads. Skinny dogs, the kings and queens of the dirt roads, scavenging for food.

An occasional glance of curiosity came from random windows and open doorways. A town that seemed all but forgotten if it wasn't for this border crossing.

Immigration was a small, stucco-walled, thatched-roof building, just like the others in town, only it had a window installed for the purpose of transacting immigration. Ceiling fans inside offered the only cooling comfort to the officer stationed there. He wasn't fussy, but actually was cheerful and helpful. I was half expecting to pay a bribe, a "special fee" for not having my "special tax form" that the officer in the north had told me I needed to exit the country. Instead, he gave us our stamp and a simple "gracias" and we were on our way toward the coast of the Usumacinta River, Paul dragging his wheeled suitcase.

There was just one lancha[13] anchored to the shore when we arrived. Two guys greeted us, asking if we wanted to go to Bethel.

Paul boarding the lancha on the Usumacinta River.

13 Small boat

GUATEMALA: "LAND OF MANY TREES"

Flores

Tikal

Antigua

GUATEMALA

Bethel, Guatemala, made Frontera Corozal look like a metropolis. It was eight streets wide and three streets deep with the main street dumping straight into or growing dustily out of the river—depending on how you wanted to look at it.

Immigration demanded we pay an entrance tax and, to avoid any potential delays in receiving our stamps, we conceded, paying the five dollars each.

In front of the almost-hidden immigration structure was a bench, and on that bench sat Gabi, an Australian-Ecuadorian woman in her mid-twenties.

"Are you headed to México?" I asked her.

"No."

"Are you waiting for a bus?"

"I'm waiting for other backpackers."

"Oh, some friends?"

"No, just anyone I can travel with."

"Oh, well, would you like to travel with us? We are headed to Tikal."

"Yes."

We proceeded with introductions, and just like that, we were now five.

The group of five, I was making the photo.

None of us talked much on the ride to Flores, the gateway city
to Tikal.

Palestina de los Altos, Guatemala, was a dusty little stop which
gave us the chance to stretch our legs, buy an ice-cold Fanta in a
glass bottle, and pick up a couple of chuchitos, a sort of tamale with
very little flavor.

I saw a vaquero[14] dismount his horse. He was lean and dirty;
his horse looked weak and saddle worn. Everything about him—
his horse, his saddle, the dirt that covered him—all of it spoke to
me. How much was a horse? How much for a saddle? Hat, boots,
harness… Yes, I was forming a plan. Buy a horse and ride across
Guatemala. I closed my eyes and dreamt of life on the range.

14 Cowboy, cattle driver

Flores

It took the Spanish one-hundred fifty-six years to conquer the final Mayan state of Flores.

The city was bustling with excitement. Perhaps the town was excited by our arrival. Flores was divided into the main city and the island of Flores. The island geared for tourists planning a trip to Tikal with its higher-priced restaurants and rooms.

Paul and I shared a room. Down the hall was a shared bathroom.

Paul hit the shower first and when he came back to the room he told me there was no hot water. I asked the owner of the house who told me the shower head was a heating device. You hit the switch and the water turned hot.

Now this device was not only hardwired into the wall; the wires were exposed. This was known as a "suicide shower." It was shocking (pun intended) that we didn't read about hundreds of backpackers dying of electrocution every year.

I jumped in, flipped the switch, and at some point during my shower, a piece of hot plastic dripped onto my back. Instinctively you'd want to reach up and shut off that which might be dripping hot plastic on you, but then you'd remember you were standing naked in a puddle of water about to touch a device with exposed electrical wires. I did what was instinctive, and my whole body vibrated with electricity.

From that day forward, it was cold showers—well, at least anywhere a Lorenzetti electric shower head was found.

Surviving electrocution, we ventured across the bridge to the main town in search of food, cerveza, and to take in a little people watching.

TIKAL

"At the Waterhole"

If you have ever seen the first *Star Wars* movie—which is really the fourth one—*A New Hope*, then you would have seen a hint of Tikal at the end where the rebel base Yavin is located.

Lunch overlooking the Great Jaguar Temple in Tikal

Enough about popular culture. We were at Tikal, home to almost ninety thousand Maya during its peak. A society that started growing in about 2000 BC; three hundred years after the legendary Biblical Flood. I was a bit of a nerd when it came to ruins like these. The fact that these cities were built with such perfection or that they were built thousands of years ago, elevating the mystery of how such large stones were transported to the site, chiseled with glyphs, and then raised to create such impressive temples.

Then it all came to an end. Many believed overpopulation was the cause of its ultimate demise. Others point to water sources becoming fouled by drought or poisoned because the Maya used cinnabar, which has mercury, to paint their buildings. The rain would wash the cinnabar off and pollute the reservoirs.

Antigua, it was agreed, was where the group should go next to take Spanish classes.

Ten hours on a Guatemalan camioneta[15] wasn't the best experience, primarily because it was uncomfortable. Remember riding the school bus? Well, that is exactly what a Guatemalan chicken bus is: an old school bus that's been pimped out with shiny reflective stickers, an abundance of colors, religious motifs, and windshields framed with strings of fuzzy dingle balls.

The name "chicken bus" immediately conjured up stories, mostly exaggerated I'm sure, from tourists who said the buses were loaded with chickens and people. Well, okay, I did see a couple people bring their chickens on board with them, and there was a pig that joined us at one time, but its name comes from the overstuffing of people on the bus like a human chicken coop.

If claustrophobia is something you have issues with, a chicken bus is not for you, although you do have the option of riding on the roof with the luggage, various bags and boxes of produce, and animals in cages. If you have trochophobia,[16] well, all the best.

---

15 Chicken Bus
16 Fear of riding on a truck or bus.

ANTIGUA

"Ancient"

Even with its population of forty-six thousand people, Antigua feels like a really quaint city, which has heavily embraced its tourism industry. Over 450 years old, its UNESCO label has helped preserve the bright-colored Spanish colonial buildings and cobblestone streets while sitting vulnerable beneath four volcanoes.

Name	Type	Last Eruption
Volcán de Acatenango	Stratovolcano	1972
Volcán de Fuego	Stratovolcano	2018
Volcán Pacaya	Complex	2021

The fourth, just south of Antigua, was Volcán de Agua, standing proudly at 12,340' high, almost as a protector of the city.

Antigua was also known for inexpensive Spanish classes, which was why we decided to come here.

I knew very little Spanish:

- hola
- de nada
- gracias
- dónde está el baño o el aeropuerto o la estación de autobuses o…

Well, you get the point.

I just needed a little more meat in my Spanglish language skills. My first one-on-one Spanish class was interesting.

The teacher was an older, portly woman, wearing traditional dress. We met at her casa and sat at a modest kitchen table in a poorly lit room, dirty dishes piled up in the sink with a picture of Jesus in the living room. She pulled out some tired children's Spanish books and started going through the process of "teaching."

"Cómo se llama," she said. I repeated. She moaned and clutched her stomach.

"¿Todo bien?" I asked.

"Sí."

She moaned and rocked back and forth. "Tengo gases estomacales." (I have stomach gas.)

I jumped in before she could follow up with "Mi llamo Jimena."

"Sí, entiendo 'come se llama,'" I said.

Moaning again, she continued to rock back and forth, only this time she actually passed the gas. Pausing, she turned a few pages in the book and then read, "Tiene los ojos azules." (She has blue eyes.)

This went on for a few minutes. "No, por favor. Habla English?" I asked. She agreed.

"I want to know things like, 'How much for the bus ticket to…?'"

Phrases I could use. I didn't care if "her eyes are blue" or "the child runs fast."

After a few hours, I paid her and decided I'd learn Spanish more organically. Gabi was fluent so I would just bounce things off her for the time being.

I've tried to pick up Spanish several times. Maybe it's just laziness on my part or maybe I truly don't have a knack for foreign languages.

My own grasp of the English language had its shortcomings because of dyslexia. When I was a kid, they dealt with dyslexia by putting you in a "resource" classroom, which was a trailer out by the playground with all the other kids with "issues." I could write, for the most part, with no problem—occasionally a number found its way into a word where a letter should be, or words like "the" ended up "hte." Reading was a constant battle, since I had to reread things over and over again. Lastly there was a struggle with word pronunciation.

In the morning, I decided to explore this colorful city. It laid out like a perfect grid, with Parque Central placed in the middle.

The intersections, if one were not paying attention, all looked the same, although they were each unique.

I checked the street names. I was at the intersection of Una Vie and Una Vie. Didn't think twice about these street names and I assumed they meant "First Ave" and "First Ave."

Most of you already know where this is going.

Turned out, just about every street in the old part of Antigua was Una Vie (one way) so every intersection had two signs reading "Una Vie" and "Una Vie." I should have remembered the name of the hostel, but I didn't. It took me forever to find it.

Every morning, before the group woke up, I would walk around town and then expand my walk into the countryside.

There was a smell in this part of the world, a sort of ongoing smell of campfire mixed in with trash and things one might consider not best for the environment, such as plastics and tyres.[17]

Ignored skinny dogs lingered the streets searching for scraps in garbage piles. Women washed stone front stoops, roosters crowed, markets prepared, uniformed kids went to school. The cool air quickly warmed with the rising sun—average day temps in the mid-seventies.

A man—a farmer, I guessed—walked his cow along the side of the road and then up a trail into the lush farmland. I followed for a while until the trail rose high enough to expose a panoramic view of the city. Only thing missing was a cup of coffee.

I met up with some other backpackers at the hostel. They were headed out for a hike and I decided to join them. Our small group took a colectivo[18] to San Vicente Pacaya, about an hour south of Antiqua.

Once there, we found the trailhead and proceeded to hike the three plus miles to the top of Volcán Pacaya, an active volcano 8373' in elevation. Ascending 1500', we reached near the top. Smoke escaping from the mountain made travel slow and visibility became limited. The smell of sulfur was strong. We made the obligatory touristy photos and returned to Antigua just in time for a siesta.

17 TBATB
18 A shared taxi (in the form of a small bus) with an established route.

After a few days, it was time for the group to disband:

- Gabi decided to go her own way, toward the coast, although she wasn't set on which coast.

- Paul had to get back home to Canada to finish school.

- Robin and Nicki were headed to South America.

I decided to email a few friends who I dove with and ask them if they wanted to meet me in Utila, Honduras, to do some diving. The responses:

"Where will we stay?"

"Is it safe? Have you been there?"

"Do they have hotels?"

Then there was an email from Beth, "I'll meet you in Caracas. Interested?"

Caracas it was. I jumped on a Tica Bus and headed toward Panama.

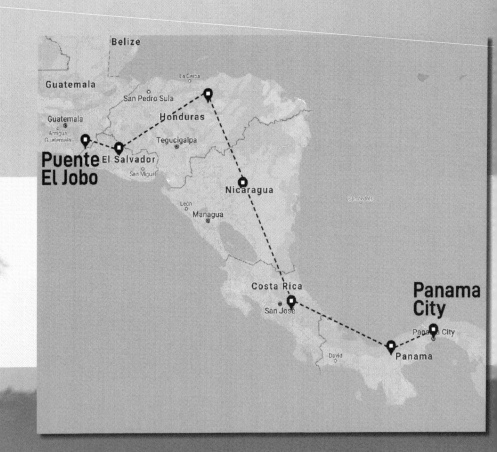

TICA BUS TO PANAMA CITY

El Salvador
Honduras
Nicaragua
Costa Rica
Panama

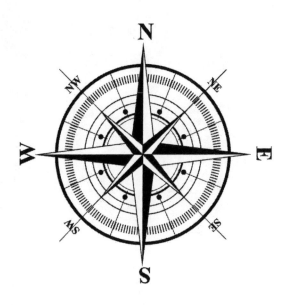

REPUBLIC OF EL SALVADOR

"The Savior"

The Tica Bus routed us through El Salvador, which arrived at the bus terminal just after dark.

Our bus driver told us it was not safe to travel at night and we would sleep here, on the bus, safely behind forty-foot-high steel walls, crowned with razor wire.

I had failed to exchange my Guatemalan quetzals for US dollars at the border, which was the newly adopted currency. While the colón was the currency of El Salvador, President Flores allowed US dollars to be used as well. My American seat neighbor, Matt, had the same problem. Plenty of quetzals, no colón or US dollars.

The security guard at the bus station told us there was an ATM just down the street and told us we were todo loco for even thinking about leaving the secure confines of the bus station and crazier for going out to get cash from an ATM.

Matt pulled out a two-foot machete and armed himself. The security guard kept watch with his submachine gun as we ventured into the darkness.

The ATM was about fifty yards away, well within eyeshot of the bus station. I inserted my card. The machine made some grinding sounds. My only hope was if the machine didn't offer up any cash, it would at least return my card.

"ENGLISH or SPANISH" the ATM screen read.

I selected ENGLISH. "BEEP."

That had to be the loudest beep I've ever heard come out of an ATM, I thought.

No doubt this alerted all the criminal elements within ear shot.

"ENTER PIN."

"BEEP, BEEP, BEEP, BEEP."

"Jesus, why is this so loud!" I looked at Matt. He held the machete like a samurai and scanned our surroundings for anyone who might be approaching.

I could see the security guard, door still open, machine gun at the ready. More grinding from the ATM. "C'mon, c'mon."

A cat ran across the street. We could hear movement down a nearby alley.

"RE-ENTER PIN."

"What!"

"BEEP, BEEP, BEEP, BEEP," followed by more grinding.

Shadows from the darkness turned into people. People who were approaching Matt and me at the ATM.

The security guard whistled and waved us back in. Perhaps he saw something he didn't like.

"C'mon… C'mon," I said to the machine.

Cash finally distributed; the card followed. We then ran for the door.

The security guard pushed us through the door, shaking his head laughing. "You gringos, estan locos."

He pulled down the solid metal security screen and closed the glass front door.

We climbed back into the bus and settled into our seats. "Well, that was stupid," I said, staring at the seat in front of me. "Yep," Matt said, putting his machete back into the overhead storage.

The sound of the bus's diesel engine starting woke me up. I told Matt I'd take care of his border crossings for helping me out.

At the border, the El Salvadoran policía charged us a departure tax, which had to be paid prior to receiving an exit stamp, and the Honduran policía kindly charged us an entrance tax in exchange for an entrada stamp.

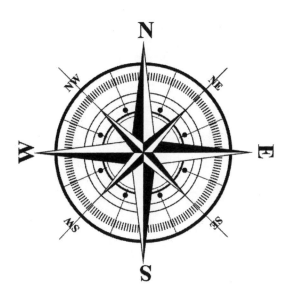

HONDURAS

"Depths"

Honduras was a boring slog of a bus ride. The most exciting thing that happened was another bus had tipped over on the Pan-American Highway, maybe in an attempt to swerve and avoid a cow. I was a bit baffled as to how this could have happened on such a flat stretch of road.

Instead of moving the bus, the locals, perhaps seventy of them, decided to get together and, armed with machetes, forge a path around the capsized bus through the shrubs lining the highway.

Disembarking the bus, I watched the organized chaos and offered some help. Help not wanted, I climbed back on the bus and read my Kerouac book that I picked up in San Francisco.[19]

After a couple of hours, we were off to Tegucigalpa, arriving mid to late afternoon.

Matt and his machete headed toward the coast to a little village he had stayed at years ago. A family had hosted him, and his plan was to return and give the family some fishing poles and gear.

I loitered at the bus estación. It would be hours before my bus to San José boarded. A young German woman, about twenty, stood alone with her backpack. It took a while for the conversation to start, but when it did, she was clear on her stance about how she felt about US Americans.

"Where did you come from?" she asked. I supposed she was asking me where I started my backpacking adventure.

"I started in the United States."

"America. I hate America and Americans," she said.

"Well, I'm a US American. Do you hate me?"

"Really? Your accent sounds like Australian," she replied.

I strongly added the US to American for a reason.

Many years ago, while traveling in Central America, a local asked where I was from. I said, "America." He responded, "I am also American from America, Central America. We are all American."

The word America comes from Martin Waldseemüller, who coined the term from Amerigo Vespucci, who mapped out South America and the Caribbean Sea around the 1500s.

Since that discussion, I have always said I am from US America.

Zee German didn't answer. She thought for a while, lit a cigarette, and turned to me.

"America takes advantage of these poor countries for profit. They are horrible."

"Really, the US takes advantage of all the countries? No other country does that?"

"Exactly."

"You're from Germany?"

"Yes."

"Do you think there are no German companies exploiting second- and third-world countries?"

"No."

"Really, is Bayer not German? What about Volkswagen? Adidas?"

I could see she was thinking and then I followed up.

"So, do you still hate me? Would you consider visiting the United States?"

"No, I don't hate you."

She stared off, watching an airplane coming in for a landing.

"Maybe. Maybe I visit United States."

The bus ride was just a few hours and the conductor decided to play *Rocky III*, at full volume with Spanish subtitles. I paid twenty-four dollars for the experience.

COSTA RICA

"Rich Coast"

Smooooth sailing for the most part.

Although immigration did give me a bit of a hassle as we entered Costa Rica, not believing the passport was mine. It took a lot of back and forth before the supervisor agreed with me that it was me in the photo, and I could proceed into their country.

PANAMA

"Abundance of Fish, Trees, and Butterflies"

C oming across the Bridge of the Americas was quite spectacular. Just the idea that this manmade object of steel and bituminous was what tied two continents together was something worthy of applause.

While crossing the bridge, looking to my right was the Gulf of Panama, leading out to the Pacific Ocean and the rest of the world. A line of ships and freighters and small crafts, like sailboats and yachts, waited their turn to enter the canal. To the left was the entrance to the canal and forward, in the distance, was the skyscraping skyline of Panama City.

I had been told the best place to buy a sailboat was in Panama. By the time couples who planned on sailing the world got to Panama, they were sick of each other and wanted to not only divorce their spouse but also the boat that got them there. I wouldn't have time to check out the yacht club. Beth would be in Caracas in just a couple of days.

The bus station in Panama City was a marvel compared to every other station I had recently visited. A taxi took me to a hostel in the

Balboa district. It was simple, clean, and family-run. I had my own room, and they offered all-day coffee.

Everything was calmer here. The hectic chaos of Central America didn't really punctuate the vernacular. A little cleaner, a little more Western perhaps.

On the bus, I created a short list of things I wanted to do while in Panama:

1. Find a bed for the next two nights. – Check
2. Buy a plane ticket to Caracas. – I jumped online for the purchase. – Check.
3. Get yellow fever vaccination.
4. Visit the Panama Canal.

I hated needles. If you wanted to draw blood, I'd rather slide on sandpaper, but I had heard a story, true or not, that a bus in Brazil was stopped by police and everyone who didn't have a yellow vaccine card was inoculated on the spot, one needle used on all those not in compliance. That was enough to encourage me to vaccinate.

Calling the US Embassy, I asked where they suggested I go to get a yellow fever vaccine. They directed me to an address at the old Howard Air Force Base, which meant I had another opportunity, actually two, to travel across the Bridge of the Americas.

It was a struggle to find the right building, as the place was in the process of completely shuttering and felt ghostly. In 1999, President Carter signed the Torrijos-Carter Treaties, which gave control of the Panama Canal back to Panama and removed the United States' presence from the area. A decision not agreed to by many, including Congressman S.I. Hayakawa, who said, "We should keep the Panama Canal. After all, we stole it fair and square."

There was only the doctor in a small room when I entered the building. She had no idea I was coming and why would she? There was no one to make my appointment.

"Hi, the US Embassy told me I can get a yellow fever vaccination here."

"They did? I think we have some vaccine. We are shutting everything down. Let me look."

I was happy to have brought my syringes that I picked up at the farmicia in México D.F. along with my antimalarial pills.

"Ah, yes, here we go." She placed the bottle on a tray and reached in a drawer for a syringe, and I was relieved to see it was still in its sterile packaging. "Now to find the WHO[20] cards."

In just five minutes, I was injected, vaccinated, documented, and out the door. Here's the proof:

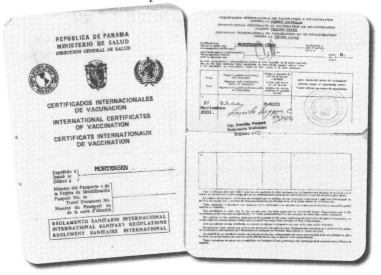

20 World Health Organization yellow card titled, "International Certificates of Vaccination."

Next stop—Panama Canal

The French, having attempted to construct the canal, failed miserably and wanted out as the project almost bankrupted the country.

So many people died under the French construction that one of the ways they funded the project was by shipping cadavers back to France and selling them for science.

The United States agreed to buy the equipment from the French but failed to negotiate control of the land with Colombia, which at the time controlled Panama.

Not taking no for an answer, President Teddy Roosevelt decided to encourage and support the Panamanians in a revolt for their sovereignty.

In 1903, the country of Panama was established, and in 1904, the United States signed a treaty with the newly formed country to build and operate the canal.

Construction of the canal started in 1880 and ended in 1914. Seventy-five thousand workers built the canal, over thirty thousand died trying.

While it might go down as one the most epic achievements of mankind, the opening of the canal received little international fanfare thanks to nineteen-year-old Gavrilo Princip. On June 28, 1914, he assassinated Archduke Ferdinand in Sarajevo, which immediately started WWI, one month prior to the canal's completion.

"NEVER BEFORE HAS MAN DREAMED OF TAKING
SUCH LIBERTIES WITH NATURE."
- Arthur Bullard

VENEZUELA: "LITTLE VENICE"

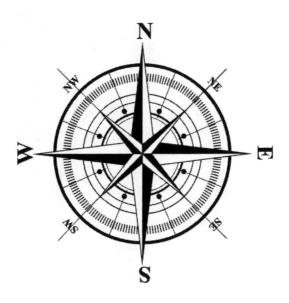

CARACAS

"Named in Honor of Santiago de León de Caracas"

The flight from Panama to Caracas was two hours long. I sat next to a doctor, Dr. Angel.

Dr. Angel shared with me his story about how he escaped from Cuba eight years ago and started a practice in Caracas. He went on about the horrors of communism and Castro's brutal regime while we drank a couple of his favorite beers, Old Milwaukee. According to the good doctor, Old Milwaukee was a popular drink in Central America.

I had been to Central America several times before, and well, I suppose I never asked for Old Milwaukee. Perhaps it was the preferred brew. I always deferred to the local brands.

Belikin

Gallo

Imperial

Cristal

I wasn't a beer snob. I drank Rolling Rock because it was trendy and Genuine Draft because it was cheap. Basically, I just wanted my beer to be cold and carbonated.

"Years ago, we had tractors. Now we have returned to using plows pulled by oxen. Bicycles are replacing cars due to gas rations. Fidel is a dangerous madman!"

His biggest regret was his inability to help his family escape. "I have not seen them since eight years now and I fear they may have been arrested or executed for my escaping."

The plane landed, and we processed through immigration. Beth, who arrived an hour before, was waiting for me. I hadn't seen her in years, and we started where we left off. Both single and good-looking, I had a little less hair. We dated for about three years in our twenties maintaining a friendship after the fact.

We spent a day in Caracas, meandering the streets, catching up, discussing what we wanted to do.

I wanted to go to Angel Falls, the highest waterfall in the world, but it would take all of her time to fly there, trek to the falls and back, and then return. Beth only had a week, and she wanted to relax a little bit before returning back to winter in the US Midwest.

We agreed to fly to Isla Margarita, known as the "Isle of Pearls" for its abundance of pearls found when Christopher Columbus arrived. Pearls still being one of its biggest industries, it was also a popular vacation destination for wealthy Venezuelans (so sayeth the woman selling us our airfare and hotel at the travel agency).

ISLA MARGARITA

We spent three days sitting on the beach, reminiscing, overall doing very little. I was anxious to run around the island and explore, but Beth was content on the beach.

I had to remind myself this was Beth's vacation, and I was just along for the ride.

Reader, I'll admit, being her copilot wasn't a tough gig. Sitting in a beach chair on Playa el Yaque with a cold Polar Pilsner soaking up the eighty-five-degree December temps was just fine with me.

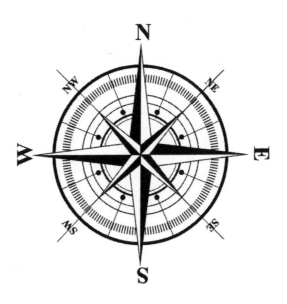

MÉRIDA

Typically, when I book a flight, I do so with all the confidence in the world of the pilot's skills. We all do.

Oh, who are we kidding? We book a ticket based off the cheapest value, expecting the very best skills in our pilot.

We saw the young-looking pilots as we boarded the ATR 42-300 turboprop plane. Max capacity—forty-eight. It reminded me a lot of the Fokker F-27 turboprops I used to load back in the early nineties working on the ramp at MSP[21] at Mesaba Airlines.

While the flight was sold to us as direct, we stopped in Valencia, ,just seventy-one miles west of Caracas—and then Barquisimeto ,roughly another one hundred miles southwest—adding a couple of hours and some more takeoff and landing experience for our pilots.

Leaving Barquisimeto, it got choppy just after takeoff. Our little plane bounced around—our flight route appeared to be straight through the Andes.

Flying through the Andes was a treat and a thrill. One minute I was looking straight out the window directly at the mountains, some rising above the plane, then moments later, we were immersed in a cloud. Mountains, clouds, repeat.

I had never had more faith in my pilots as I did that day. My only hope was that these pilots had the same skills and experience as my dad—making every maneuver with great thought, making no assumptions, and lacking any and all complacence.

Then again, I put my life in the hands of a company that offered me the best deal. What should I expect for negotiating my safety for a few dollars?

Alberto Carnevalli Airport in Mérida was a single runway airport sitting 5400' up in the mountains and prohibits night operations due to its complexity on approach and takeoff. Twelve years after we successfully arrived and departed Mérida, Flight 518 to Caracas slammed into the mountain killing all forty-six people onboard.

Beth and I did some of the "must do" things *Lonely Planet* suggested. The two most memorable being the ride up El Teleférico de Mérida, which was not only the highest cable car in the world, reaching an altitude of 15,633', but also the second longest at over seven and a half miles.

Now reader, keep in mind, we had just arrived from sea level and were now at an ear-popping altitude of 15,633'.

There are three distinct defined levels of altitude:

High altitude:	4900' – 11,500'
Very high altitude:	11,500' – 18,000'
Extreme altitude:	18,000' +

At "very high altitude," where we currently were, the following could occur:

- Difficulty sleeping
- Difficulty eating and digesting food

- Risk of high-altitude pulmonary edema (HAPE), which is when fluid fills the lungs
- Risk of high-altitude cerebral edema (HACE), which is when fluid penetrates the blood-brain barrier, leading to coma and ultimately death

With the amount of time we would end up spending at the top of Pico Espejo, none of the above mentioned would be an issue, but this would not be my last time to the top of the Teleférico.

It was a struggle to breathe when we arrived and exited the cable car; however, there wasn't that far to wander. The peak offered a rugged sharp ridge and lifeless terrain. A faded trail led northeast but didn't look safe.

The views were amazing. It seemed like the Andes didn't stop.

Five thousand five hundred miles in length, from north to south, Los Andes would be my home for the next few months. I would cross over and over again as I weaved ever southward to an unspecified destination.

Beth and I took obligatory pictures, leaning into the intense wind that tried to blow us off the steep edge.

South America, if I were to base this first "extreme" tourist destination on, took a less "nanny state" approach to safety. More was invested in common sense than railings.

Just north of where we stood was Pico Bolívar, named after the hero of South America, Simón José Antonio de la Santísma Trinidad Bolívar y Ponte Palacios or simply Simón Bolívar, El Libertador.

Simón Bolívar was an epically important leader who freed Venezuela, Bolivia, Colombia, Ecuador, Perú, and Panama from the

Spanish Empire. Pico Bolívar was the highest peak in Venezuela. A name well deserved for such an important man.

I didn't know it yet, but in a few days, I would be on my way to summit Pico Bolívar. For now, Beth and I had more important matters. Descend back to Mérida and stop at Heladería Coromoto, an ice cream parlor, which according to *Lonely Planet* and *Guinness World Records*, offered a record breaking 850 flavors of ice cream, which included, but was not limited to:

Vermouth

Perro Caliente (Hot Dog)

Arroz con Queso (Rice with Cheese)

Huevos Chimbos (Egg sweet bread)

Camarones al Vino (Shrimp and wine)

Salmon

I didn't like ice cream, but when in Rome, I opted for a scoop of Menta Chip and tried a scoop of the whiskey flavor, which surprisingly tasted like whiskey.

Hanging low and just walking the streets of Mérida with absolutely no agenda was how Beth and I spent our last days together.

I made sure she safely got on the plane back to Caracas and then stayed a while in Mérida to figure out my next destination. I had no real agenda aside from continuing to head south. At some point I'd run out of land and have to start heading north but that was a ways away.

After seeing her off at the airport, I headed back to the hostel where I met Edward, an Ecuadorian student studying at

La Universidad de Los Andes. We hit it off immediately. Over a few beers, he asked if I was interested in doing a few activities with him before he headed home to Ecuador for Christmas. Without asking him what these activities were, I said yes.

Activity one was paragliding.

Edward knew a guy who he went to university with who had a company that took people paragliding. The next thing I knew I was strapped into a tandem harness running down a steep slope with my pilot, Sabastian, until we had lift off.

This was different than skydiving. This was a mixture of soaring like an eagle and floating like a cloud. It was peaceful; time stood still. The higher we were, the slower the world spun underneath us. As we closed in on terra firma, it felt like we were traveling at one hundred miles per hour as we skirted the tree line.

The mountains stood grand, timeless, unconcerned as they watched us swoop and sweep along their contours. The wind played with our parachute. Sabastian understood its language, and we danced and made lazy shapes in the sky for forty-five minutes. It was incredible and over all too soon.

Activity two was to summit Pico Bolívar. We took a day to pret pare, gather gear, and talk with our guide about what to expect. I still had my tent, sleeping bag, and air mattress from my cycling trip.[22]

Our guide would bring food, ropes, harnesses, and helmets.

---

22 Did I mention you should read *The Buddha and the Bee* if you haven't?

PICO BOLÍVAR

Day 1

We took the Teleférico to the top of Pico Espejo just after noon. The guide led us north along the ridge on a lightly used rugged, steep trail, which I deemed dangerous when I saw it the first time. The trail dropped down on the east side of the ridge line turning into a steep, off-camber line complicated with loose scree. Every step was slow and deliberate, very little room for error. With the challenging terrain, hiking with gear, and approaching sixteen thousand feet in elevation, the hike to Campamento Albornoz en la Base was just a couple of miles but took hours.

Campamento Albornoz en la Base was simply the flattest bit of earth available on the side of the mountain closest to Pico Bolívar. The ridge of the Andes cut off the sunlight early, and we all happily crawled into our tents.

At very high altitude, it takes water less time to boil. The higher you go, the lower the boiling point becomes. At sea level, water boils at 212 degrees Fahrenheit. At ten thousand feet, it boils at 194 degrees F. This is great if making, let's say coffee or soup broth. But since the boiling water temperature is lower, it actually takes longer to cook food.

When it was time to eat, I could barely get out of my tent. The altitude was hitting me hard. I couldn't eat a bite, much less sip down some hot tea. To make things worse I didn't sleep at all that night. Both of these were symptoms of very high altitude. Edward was in the same boat. I could see him looking dazed and confused trying to sip down hot tea.

Day 2

When we woke up, the sun was up but hidden behind the clouds, which we found ourselves engulfed in. I had a terrible headache and tried to sip down more tea our guide had prepared, but it was a struggle. He handed me some breakfast, but I couldn't keep anything down. Leaving the tents and sleeping bags at base camp, we put on our harnesses and helmets and headed to the top with our guide carrying one hundred feet, plus or minus, of climbing rope and other climbing equipment needed, in case of an emergency, I suspect.

The trail to the face of the peak was along a one-thousand-foot cliff.

Now reader, before I go on, I'd like to share with you something. I have what the French call, *l'appel du vide*. In English this translates to *the call of the void*.

In height situations, I have a strong impulse to hurl myself into the void. It's a dangerously uncontrollable urge, and according to some research I have done on the matter, it's concluded that urges like jumping from heights, the desire to swerve head on into another car, or cutting yourself are simply due to some mis-wiring in the brain. I don't want to die, so it's the animal survival instinct inside us that prevents that, but sometimes the mind is stronger. At least it feels that way, hence the struggle.

The upside was clouds had closed in moments after we started along the one-thousand-foot cliff trail. This took the whole heights thing out of the equation, as I could no longer see the void.

An hour or so later, we reached the base of the face of the peak itself. It might have been two hours. I was in a total daze. Drool hung from my lip and snot from my nose. I felt like my eyeballs were going to explode from the pressure of being so high.

Moving was even slower now as we ascended. Two steps, catch your breath. Another two steps, another need to rest. Just raising your head to look up required time to catch your breath.

Just two hundred feet from the peak, we came across three climbers who were ahead of us. As we pressed up the face, they created a rockslide. Edward and the guide were ten feet above me and managed to get out of the way, while the only escape that I saw from the rocks and chunks of ice heading my way was to let go and drop into a small crack. I crunched down in this protective shelter for a good five minutes and decided I didn't need to see the bust of Simón Bolívar atop Pico Bolívar and told the guide I was heading down.

I untied from the safety rope and started down to base camp. Should I have untied from the safety rope? Absolutely not. Was I thinking straight? Absolutely not.

The upside was I was heading down; the downside was the clouds had cleared and I had a real true sense of my location. I was on a steep face of a mountain and below me was an eighty-foot descent straight down a narrow "chimney."[23] I didn't remember this part of the ascent, but the clouds were thick, visibility was limited, and the altitude was having a powerful effect on my thought process.

After completing the descent, I stood at the base of the chimney and could make out the thousand-foot cliff trail that led me back to the tents. Then I passed out, for exactly how long, I don't recall. Edward and the guide had not caught me so perhaps a minute, perhaps twenty. Long enough for the clouds to fill in the void and give me safe passage back to the tents.

Edward and the guide returned just as dark was setting in. Dinner was prepared, but I couldn't eat. That evening, I hardly slept a wink although I was physically drained.

Preparing to ascend Pico Bolívar.

23 A crack in the rock large enough for the body to shimmy up or down.

Day 3

There is a saying, "Horses trot faster back to the barn." I don't really know if that is a saying—maybe I just made it up.

We woke up, crammed our gear clumsily into our packs, and headed back to the Teleférico, hoping to time it perfectly and simply just load up on one that was waiting for our arrival. It didn't turn out as perfectly, but it was just an hour wait before we were descending back to an elevation agreeable to our animal species. I could feel the pressure in my eyeballs alleviate and my headache start to diminish. After thirty minutes back at 5400', my appetite returned and Edward and I found a pizza place.

I stared at Edward and thought, the next time this dude asks me to do something, I'm going to research it first.

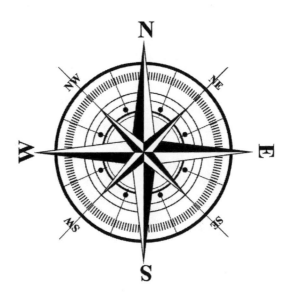

BACK IN MÉRIDA

The next morning, after a solid sleep, I checked my email. It was the middle of December and there was a notice from my credit union with an alarming message. Effective Jan. 1, 2002, a new debit card would be sent to replace my current one. Apparently, there was a hack, and all credit union members were to receive a new debit card.

Now this was problematic as my debit card was my only way to get money. I emailed a message asking if I could be excluded from this event, and the response was "NO."

Now, what was your hero[24] to do? First thing was to pull out a few hundred dollars' worth of Venezuelan bolivars. Finding an ATM, I inserted my card and punched in my PIN. The machine churned, my card was ejected, and I placed it back in my pocket. I could hear the cash preparing to eject. Just then, someone behind me jammed what I thought was a gun in my back and said in a heavy Spanish accent, "Give me your money." The cash ejected partway, and I turned around to see Edward messing with me.

"You are a pendejo!"[25]

He laughed. "Come, get your cash. There are problems with the government. Let's leave town."

24 TBATB
25 "Asshole" in Spanish

As I turned to reach for my money, the ATM swallowed it up. Apparently, there was a time limit on how long your cash would sit in the jaws of the dispensing machine. I re-inserted the card, re-entered the PIN, and extracted the same amount. Later I found the credit union had recorded this as two transactions, deducting both from my account, which they later corrected.

That night, the town erupted. Hugo Chávez had come out on TV and declared something to the effect that he will be president of Venezuela until 2020 after rewriting the constitution or maybe because of the $0.03 bus fare increase, not really sure.

Tyres were soon rolled into the middle of the streets, piled high, and lit on fire. Rocks and bottles were thrown at the military. In turn, the military forces worked to control the situation with tear gas, smoke grenades, soldiers in full tactical gear, and armored military vehicles. This show of force did not detour the well-organized students, it only prolonged the situation. The smell of burning tyres and tear gas was heavy. My eyes were burning and it was difficult to breathe. I watched it all from a side street with a few other strangers and decided that maybe Edward was right, we should get out of town.

The day after Hugo Chávez's declaration, the Venezuelan people responded by shutting down the entire country in protest. All businesses, transportation, everything.

Chávez's response? Something to the effect of, "Today I declare a national holiday. No one has to work."

If you don't like the conversation, change it.

LOS LLANOS

E dward arranged for him and me to go to Los Llanos for a few days until things settled down. I wasn't sure exactly what was up with the arrangements Edward made, but early the next morning, a guy pulled up in a 1982 Toyota Land Cruiser. Inside were a young Dutch couple and an Australian traveling solo. We drove for six backbreaking hours along dirt roads to our destination.

To this day, I still don't know where that was exactly. I just know I was somewhere in Los Llanos, which I thought was a town. Turns out, Los Llanos means "The Plains" and covers 145,000 square miles of land, reaching almost the entire length of Venezuela and well into Colombia.

Along the way, at a police control point, our driver was ticketed for not having a list of names and passport numbers of all the occupants in his Land Cruiser. I'm sure it was worked out with a bribe, and we were soon on our way.

I thought about my bike trip. The freedom I had to ride my bicycle across the United States[26] through cities and towns and counties without the need to answer questions about why I was doing it, where I was going, or identification to prove who I was.

Before reaching the final destination, we stopped at a mercado, which was attached to a bar at the intersection of two remote dirt roads and had a group of drunk old men drinking beers in the hot sun.

"If you want anything like snacks or beer or liquor or to buy some film for your cameras, here is your chance. There will be food for dinner and breakfast while you are there."

I still didn't know where "there" was but I wanted to stretch my legs. With my debit card expiring within the month, I refrained from spending money on things I didn't need, like beer.

While I waited for the rest of the group to collect their provisions, one of the old drunk guys approached me. He was heavyset, smelled of sweat and warm beer, and had a permanent smile on his face. He spoke to me only in Spanish and decided it was his duty to wet his thumb with his beer and bless me on the forehead several times with the sign of the cross.

I was now protected from all the evils that awaited me here in the Venezuelan prairies.

The amazing thing about Los Llanos was the abundant wildlife. There were animals everywhere.

It was clear we were on some sort of unlicensed or unapproved tour, but it didn't feel that way. The lack of organization made it feel more like, "I know a guy who will take us to his grandmother's farm in the middle of nowhere for a week, and if you want, we can pay him gas money to drive there and do stuff."

It was a new adventure. I liked the Australian guy. I didn't much care for the Dutch guy, but his girlfriend was young and very attractive. Something she was fully aware of, as she liked to show more than was necessary. Of course, Edward, the Aussie, and I didn't object.

The destination was a few simple structures surrounded by an electric fence. Children ran up as we approached, excited to see who was packed in the back of the Toyota.

We would spend the next few nights in one of the buildings with hammocks, which was really no different than the owner's residence. The difference was they had a TV and an indoor bathroom.

The hammocks were more than comfortable, and I learned the trick was to sleep sideways in the hammock. It keeps your back straight rather than curved.

I was still recovering from the Pico Bolívar hike and was enjoying the now thousand-foot elevation and the warmer temperature, hovering in the low nineties during the height of the day.

Breakfast was a simple event: some eggs, homemade bread, and coffee at a picnic table. Dishes were washed in a fifty-gallon barrel with a hose at the bottom, which also served to hose down the area after meals. A makeshift water tower caught rainwater and could be filled manually by climbing up and down the ladder with buckets of water.

The owner offered up their horses. I was the only one who opted to take one out. Did they ask if I knew how to ride a horse? No. Did they ask if I knew where to go or how to get back from wherever it was I might find myself? No.

They just brought out a saddled horse and off I went. Exploring. Were there dangers afoot? Perhaps, but nothing I was aware of or told about, so I thought nothing of it. Just stayed on the horse and out of any deep water, or shallow water for that matter—there were anacondas and crocodiles playing.

It was a great day just riding, with the occasional gallop. At one point, I had her running just to prove to myself I could do it. I thought about my idea of buying a horse and saddle back in Guatemala and riding into Honduras—what a missed opportunity. Maybe on the way back.

Returning back to camp, the Dutch couple were still in their hammocks, reading books. The Aussie took off someplace with Edward, so I returned the horse and played fútbol with the children and their deflated ball.

That evening, we went out with one of the ranch workers looking for an anaconda that they claimed was picking off their livestock.

The green anaconda is the largest, with an average length of twenty feet and weighing 150 pounds. So if we happened to actually come across one, I wasn't exactly sure what the endgame was going to be, aside from perhaps a swift beheading with the rancher's machete. It seemed pointless, as I was sure many anacondas lived in these marshes. I went anyway, mostly out of curiosity.

Indigenous people of South America have several myths regarding the anaconda.

In Colombia, some believe the anaconda to be a reflection of the Milky Way, which descended to earth and created the Amazon, the river where all humans emerged. Some Ecuadorians believe it guards the doorway to heaven.

The farmer waded in chin-deep waters with a stick and a flash-light. I stood comfortably and safely on the dirt road on the edge of the swamp. Actually, I'm pretty sure I was closer to the center of the road on the off-chance anacondas could fly and preferred light-er-skinned humans.

Although we didn't find an anaconda, a quick scan of the water with the flashlight lit up a slurry of glowing eyes from mammals and reptiles alike, looking for their next meal.

"THE ENEMY HAS US SURROUNDED!
THEY WON'T GET AWAY THIS TIME!!"
— *Chesty Puller*

My only protection from all this nature was a rancher six inches shorter than me who was armed with a stick and a flashlight.

I was happy to return empty-handed, but I was less than happy to return to find a six-foot anaconda moving slowly across camp under the picnic table. The rancher decided he wanted to terminate the serpent and turned to me with a smile.

"You want to help remove skin. Cut up snake? We use meat for hunt."

"Uh, I'm good, happy to watch, maybe fetch you a beer."

He then dragged it by its tail toward the far end of the com-pound where they processed most of their food.

After dinner, we settled into our hammocks. With no electricity in the hammock room, you needed a head lamp to read, but I soon found that to be a bad idea as it attracted so many bugs. So I shut off my lamp and closed my eyes, falling asleep to the Los Llanos symphony.

Sometime in the night, I had to pee. I headed to the outhouse barefoot and with my headlamp. Little eyes glowed around me. Dozens and dozens of giant toads littered the grounds. I navigated around them as I entered the outhouse where a giant toad sat on a ledge staring at me. I pissed and it spit, or perhaps its tongue shot out at me, or worse yet, it might have pissed on me.

I thought about the 1972 movie *Frogs* featuring a young mustache-less Sam Elliott. It was a horror movie I watched as a kid about a rich southern plantation owner whose family wreaks havoc on the environment only to have nature get its final revenge.

I made an effort to piss before going to bed, and if need be, hold it until morning. I didn't shit for three days as I took no comfort in the thought of sitting over a dark pit harboring unknown entities of any dimension.

Aside from breakfast, I laid in my hammock most of the day reading. The Aussie offered me a beer, which turned into two, and then Edward shared some of his rum. My reading session turned into a nap.

As dusk approached, we all went out for a hike along a dirt road that divided the marshes. The rancher gave us each a three-foot long stick with a piece of fishing line about twelve feet long and a hook. With him was a bucket of cut-up anaconda from the day before. We were going to catch piranha. It didn't take much to draw the piranha toward us. The rancher threw in a couple pieces of raw meat and the water quickly turned into a slurry of activity. I dropped my hook in the water, and in a matter of seconds, the meat was gone and the hook was empty.

From then on, the rancher smiled and told me to jerk the pole when the water starts churning. The trick was not so much to catch the fish, but rather to snag one, perhaps in the side or belly, wherever. After that bit of instruction, it was bam, bam, bam. I pulled out eight-nine-ten piranha in quick succession. The others in the group each caught their share as well. Our bucket was full of piranha, gasping and floundering until they took their last breath.

Fresh catch of piranha

To chum the waters, the rancher threw a portion of the snake meat out far from shore. Something was lurking under the water. Attaching another piece of meat on a four-inch three-pronged hook that was attached to a nylon rope, he tossed it out into the marsh. In no time at all, the rancher was struggling with the rope. He hooked something, and it was not in the best of moods.

Me and the Aussie jumped in and grabbed the line.

We were fighting a crocodile. It was fascinating how strong this reptile was. Just three, maybe four feet long, it put up an intense fight only to lose in the end. Dinner was crocodile and piranha.

I didn't care for the crocodile. I have had alligator, and it was equally as tough, requiring a lot of seasoning. The piranha was not something I'd order seconds of.

The evening was spent discussing our hunt and sharing Edward's rum. Lucky for all of us, he brought two bottles.

Our last day, I helped around the compound, doing chores. The owners pushed back, but I wanted to be productive, and they finally gave in. The afternoon involved swinging in the hammock, finishing my book, and helping Edward finish his rum.

Heading back toward Mérida, the road peacefully rose back up into the Andes. The lower elevation was lush and green. We stopped at a wonderful little river to swim. A twenty-foot-long slab of rock made for a wonderful natural slide. Having not bathed in days, the plunge was refreshing.

I explored above the slide, along the river, and came across what appeared to be some sort of occultic ceremonial goings on.

The outline of two bodies was marked out on the ground. Well-used colored candles were placed randomly around the outlines and upon stones, earth, and branches. A piece of paper was set under a small stone. I called up our guide who read the paper. He told me they were directions on human sacrifice and included items needed to complete the ceremony. He looked around to see if anyone was watching us and suggested we not touch anything and perhaps pack up and continue on.

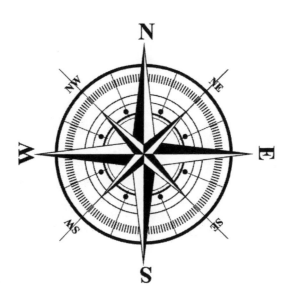

BACK IN MÉRIDA

I t was cold and raining, a perfect day to start a new book, maybe do a little journaling.

Late in the day, a French guy pulled up to the hostel on his BMW motorcycle. Having a BMW motorcycle parked at home in my garage, it was almost a duty that I engage my motorcycle brethren. For I had ridden many adventurous miles around the United States, and I was prepared to tell him all my experiences and offer unsolicited advice.

That was until he informed me that he had been riding around the world on his motorcycle for the past five years and just came across the Darién Gap by ship. I was humbled. The longest motorcycle trip I ever took was two weeks in my homeland filled with what I could only imagine was less than interesting stories for the Frenchman.

Apparently not his first time in Mérida, he had been riding around the Andes and had left some gear here that he was collecting.

I suddenly missed my bicycle and was very much inspired to buy a motorcycle.

"Do you want to have a beer?"

"Yes, yes I do." I wanted to hear about his adventures, though he wasn't big on wanting to talk about them. His interest was going out and getting a little altered.

I put down my book and threw on my sweater, and we grabbed a taxi. He took me to a hangout he had visited here before. A whisper into the bouncer's ear combined with a handshake full of cash produced a bag of shrooms. The Frenchman looked at me and winked.

"C'mon. Let's have beer."

We went inside, sat at a table, and chased the shrooms down with a beer. It was still pretty early by Venezuelan standards. Bars didn't typically get ripping until about nine p.m. It was around seven if I had to guess. I was still without a watch.

It was a slow burn of a night. A few students shared our table, and once they learned I was from the United States, they began to tell me of all the failings of capitalism. The mural on the wall opposite me actually had the key points highlighted, showing the US American Flag on the left and the flag of Venezuela on the right. Above them read:

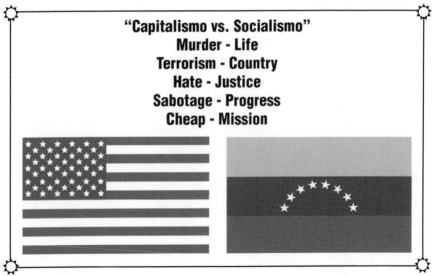

"Capitalismo vs. Socialismo"
Murder - Life
Terrorism - Country
Hate - Justice
Sabotage - Progress
Cheap - Mission

I could see their point on several topics, although I didn't necessarily agree. I was outnumbered, and frankly, trying to explain to them that had it not been for capitalism, I wouldn't have the financial freedom to aimlessly travel around the Americas, seemed futile.

I doubted they would understand. No, their philosophy was written on the wall, literally.

For them, it was "¡Trabajadores del mundo, únanse!" and "De cada uno según su capacidad, a cada uno según sus necesidades."

Translated into English: "Workers of the world, unite!" and "From each according to his ability, to each according to his needs."

Other revolutionary images and slogans decorated the walls; the communist flag and overused portrait of Che hung most prominently.

"IRONY: YOU SPEND YOUR ENTIRE LIFE COMBATING

THE FORCES OF CAPITALISM, ONLY TO END UP ON A

T-SHIRT SOLD AT THE GAP."[27]

— meme

The mushrooms were starting to kick in. Another beer was brought to me, although I don't recall ordering it. The French guy was mingling with some girls and pointed over to me. One of them gave me a cheeky smile. I sat listening to the students at our table discussing something very intensely in Spanish. I wondered where this second beer came from and watched things become very vivid. I stared at Lenin and started giggling.

27 Trendy clothing chain in the United States.

Growing up in the 1970s and 80s, it was "Better dead than red." Russians were bad, nay evil. Sting was so concerned he wrote the song "Russians" with the line "I hope the Russians love their children too."

When the United States hockey team beat the Soviets in the 1980 Olympics, it was like a war was being fought and we just won a huge ideological battle. It was celebrated as "The Miracle on Ice." Then the Era of Stagnation came to an end with Gorbachev, and in 1989, the Iron Curtain fell. "The Wall" came down, and on December 26, 1991, the USSR was no longer.

If these students did experience life in a capitalistic society where they could own property and create their own wealth without limits, would it change their opinions of it?

"ALL SYSTEMS ARE CAPITALIST. IT'S JUST A MATTER
OF WHO OWNS AND CONTROLS THE CAPITAL..."
– *Ronald Reagan*

The girls and French guy took me dancing later that evening. Somehow, I made it back to the hostel before the sun came up. The details of how that happened remain a mystery.

Late the next morning, I purchased a plane ticket back to Caracas and onward to Quito. Edward invited me to spend Christmas with his family in Quito, so I opted to skip Colombia, promising myself I would return another time.

Arriving in Caracas, I had to claim my bags and then head back to the ticket counter to check in and be processed through immigration. As I approached the counter, a man approached me, asking if I wanted to have my backpack wrapped in plastic.

Not all encounters when traveling were negative but along the line of "Fool me once, shame on you; fool me twice, shame on me."

My guard was up. I became a bit more cynical and leery of almost any offer of service, and as a gringo, I had to accept the fact that I was a target. The question was, would I be a victim?

"No, I'm good, thanks."

"Are you sure? It is only five US dollars."

I looked him up and down. "No, really. The pack is all beat up. I don't care if it gets dirtier than it already is. But thank you."

He laughed. "No, no, no. It's not to protect the bag from dirt. The people who load the bags into the plane sometimes smuggle drugs in people's bags. The plastic makes it harder for them to do that."

"You're shitting me. Well, here's five bucks, wrap away."

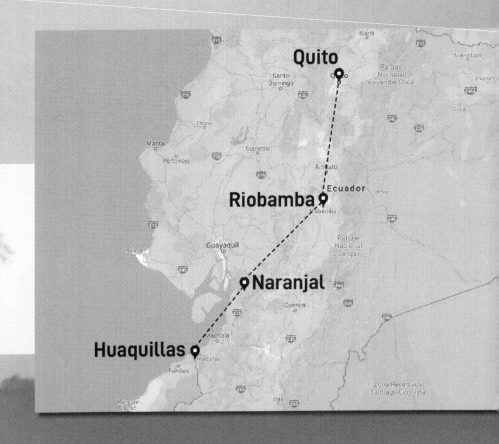

ECUADOR: "EQUATOR"

QUITO

L anding in Quito was a massive clusterfuck. I didn't know how
   something as simple as debarking a plane and picking up luggage could turn into a swarm of chaos. It must be said that the "old"
Mariscal Sucre International Airport, which I had just landed at, was
not only busting at the seams, but at the time was one of the busiest
airports in South America, handling over six million passengers a
year. Many passengers, it appeared, were flying for the first time. My
advantage was my height as the typical Ecuadorian was only 5'4". I
could see over the mass of people as I waited in immigration to get
my stamp.

I had spent a lot of time in airports. As the son of a pilot, I
took full advantage of the perks the airlines offered their employees and family. I had the passcode to the crew lounge for Republic
Airlines—formally North Central, later acquired by Northwest, now
owned by Delta.

Republic Airlines' crew lounge code in the 1980s? 1-2-3-4.

The word "lounge" conjures up some luxurious place with chan-
deliers and champagne. Fact is, it was a rather unattractive place
that had a small TV mounted in a corner displaying live national
weather conditions, a beat-up p-lam counter where pilots would get
their flight information, and metal shelves holding flight bags, each

made unique by a sticker of the equipment the pilot flew or their initials embossed below the handle.

Those were different times: smoking and non-smoking sections on planes, cockpit doors were left open, and if you scored an aisle seat, you could watch the takeoff and landing through the cockpit window. Mid-flight, pilots would wander down the aisle shaking hands with the passengers, handing out plastic wings to kids, and sharing smiles. I once got to sit in the copilot's seat during a flight, and scored the jump seat a few times, which was a little-known seat that allowed an extra person to sit in the cockpit.

One of the great perks of being the son of a commercial pilot was flying non-revenue or non-rev. I could grab a ticket, write in the departing airport and destination airport, and off I went.

The downside of flying non-rev was that I could only get on the plane if there happened to be an extra seat left. If there were four non-revs waiting to board, it went by the date of hire. My dad's hire date gave me a leg up, but Dad was very strict about this. If there was a pilot or flight attendant in uniform and I was offered the seat before them because of his hire date, I would, without question, give the seat to the uniformed crew member. If I wasn't able to get on the last flight of the day, I slept on the floor or on a bench. I bought food from vending machines with the $0.25 return refunds I collected from returning luggage carts. It was a lot of fun being in the airport at night with just the cleaning crew. A sort of teenage version of Mehran Karimi Nasseri.[28]

---

28 Iranian refugee who lived in Charles de Gaulle Airport from August 1988 until July 2006.

Non-rev also meant I had to wear a button-up shirt, tie, dress shoes, and slacks. I was eighteen when my dad stopped giving me passes. The first flight I took paying full fare I wore flip flops, shorts, and a t-shirt. A practice I continue to this day.

Edward disappeared at immigration. As a citizen, he was able to skip the "gringo" line and headed for the doors. Whether or not he ditched me on purpose so as to not have to pay me back the ten dollars I gave him at the airport in Caracas or the mob swallowed him up and we simply disconnected really didn't matter. My only disappointment was missing out on an authentic Ecuadorian Christmas with his family.

As it stood, I was going to be alone for Christmas.

The gauntlet of taxi drivers congregated and aggressively pursued all those who exited el aeropuerto, but gringos like me were an easy target and a triple charge.

The words, "My friend, you need taxi," and, "Come with me, very cheap," repeated in a round.

I always sought out the taxi driver least interested. Sometimes sleeping in his car. In Latin America, taxi driving was a male-dominated sport.

I found myself at a makeshift hostel, guided there by my *Lonely Planet: South America on a Shoestring* guidebook. It was an abandoned university that rented out their dorm rooms by the night.

The place was sterile and empty. No doubt I was the only person there aside from the student who showed me to my dorm bed and the silhouette of a janitor. Or perhaps the ghost of a janitor who now wandered the halls after an accidental death of an exploding boiler. Either way, I never saw it or him again.

Day one was hammering out a couple of chores. First things first, I went to the US Embassy to get pages added to my passport. As it stood, immigration officers were stamping stamps over stamps in my passport, and I was thinking about visiting Brazil, which required two empty pages for the visa.

The US Embassy had a line around it of Ecuadorians trying to get visas to travel to the United States.

> "A SIMPLE WAY TO TAKE MEASURE OF A COUNTRY IS
> TO LOOK AT HOW MANY WANT IN AND HOW MANY
> WANT OUT."
> — *Tony Blair*

I approached the guard booth at the embassy.

"Is this the line to get into the embassy?"

"Sir, are you a citizen of the United States?"

"Yes, yes, I am. I was just getting in line…"

"That line is for non-citizens, sir. Please, come with me."

"Really?"

"Yes, what is the nature of your business?"

"Passport, I ran out of pages."

"Please, follow me."

He brought me to a small waiting room. No one else was in there. A woman behind the counter and a wall of bulletproof glass asked what I needed.

"Passport pages, I heard I can have pages added to my passport."

"Sure, I can do that for you. Please have a seat."

She took my passport and returned less than ten minutes later. My passport had doubled in thickness. Amazing. I thought I would be here all day.

I found a taxi driver who agreed to take me to a few motorcycle shops in town. Even the used motorcycle were expensive. Finally, I had him drop me off at a bar, where I enjoyed a few beers and hammered out my next move. My next move was the internet café next door.

After composing a status email to friends and family, I thought about things I wanted to do.

- Buy a motorcycle – too expensive
- Buy a bicycle – eh
- Run a marathon – there it was

I had run marathons before, so I searched for marathons happening this time of year in South America. Marathon running wasn't as big in South America, so the options were slim pickings but one stuck out: Antarctica Marathon–March 2002.

The marathon was sold as a package, which in a nutshell was as follows:

- Depart country of origin
- Group arrives in Buenos Aires
- Group flies to Ushuaia and boards ship
- Ship goes to Antarctica and returns to Ushuaia
- Group flies back to Buenos Aires then onto their country of origin

After a few back-and-forth emails, the race director agreed to discount my cost if I met them in Ushuaia, charging me for just the voyage by sea, across the Drake Passage.

Seven days, six nights: $2,800.

It was a hefty chunk of change, but I pulled the trigger. I mean, it's Antarctica. I had three months to get to Ushuaia and more than enough time to train. My days were pretty empty. What else was I going to do?

The marathon gave me a goal, something to strive for. A destination, a timeline. One could only roam without purpose for so long. Our nature was to be productive, contribute in some way. I hadn't done much of that over the past few months, but then I thought about life before the bike trip, before the bus to México, and further on south to my present location, how did this happen?

Back on the streets, I found an open street market, which offered everything from alpaca blankets to spatulas to DVD players to fried goods to bootlegged CDs.

A Chilean band by the name of La Ley was currently all the rage.

"¿Tiene La Ley?" I asked the bootleg CD vendor.

"¿Cómo?"

"¿La Ley? ¿Tiene?" Was I asking this wrong?

"¿Cómo?"

"¿La Ley! ¿Tiene La Ley?"

"No entiendo."

"¿La Ley?"

I didn't know how many different ways I could say La Ley.

I shuffled though the CDs and, sure enough, found a La Ley CD and showed the vendor.

"Ohhh, La Ley… Sí, tengo La Ley."

I also grabbed Blink 182, Green Day, and Manu Chao.

Pages added to passport – done.

Beers consumed – done.

Motorcycle purchase – on hold.

Marathon registration – done.

I jumped on a local bus that I was told would lead me to another bus that would take me to the Mitad del Mundo.

On the bus, I found a seat next to a professionally dressed woman somewhere in her fifties and asked if I could sit next to her.

"You are American?"

"Yes."

"Why are you here?" She seemed annoyed.

"What?! Oh I don't know. I suppose I just decided to travel, and I suppose I just happened to find myself here, on this bus, next to you, in Quito."

"Ah, America!" She raised her arms in the air and looked up, as if praying to a higher power. "Why would you want to leave to come here? Why would anyone want to leave!? It is the Garden of Eden! I hope one day to live there."

"Well, it's definitely got its perks, but the world is big and I'm just taking it all in."

She shook her head disapprovingly. "If I lived in America, I would never leave. God made America. It is heaven on earth."

"Have you been?"

"Yes, just once."

"Have you tried to become a citizen?"

"Yes, I tried once and was denied."

"Why not try again?"

"We can only try twice, and then you can never try again. I have decided not to try ever again."

"Why?"

"Because if I am denied again, I know I will never be able to live in America. But if I never apply, I can live my life knowing one day I could become a citizen."

She was a lawyer, one of the first female lawyers to manage a law firm in Ecuador. She had only one dream in her life and that was, in case you hadn't guessed, to return to and live in the United States.

It's a crap shoot in the wheel of life, isn't it? Two random people connect, have sex, and boom, there you are. Born in a clean hospital, or a hut in Mongolia. Rich or oppressed, blind or with sight. Healthy or with cancer.

I supposed in the scheme of things, aside from my receding hairline, I was pretty lucky. White, male, stunningly handsome, sort of smart, healthy enough to have biked from Minneapolis to Truckee, and born in a country that offered a passport, giving me access to almost any country in the world.

You learned very quickly that you literally "jump off the bus" in Quito. It might slow down to three to five miles per hour, but stopping—stopping only happens when an elderly woman was getting on or off out of respect. It was also expected that if a woman got on a bus, no matter how old, the male would, without a second thought, give up their seat. At least in 2001, that was how it was.

MITAD DEL MUNDO

"Middle of the World"

M itad del Mundo was a giant monolithic monument with a sphere on top standing ninety-eight feet tall, put there by the French, albeit in the wrong place. This little detail, for the most part, was unknown to most, if not all, of the tourists who came to straddle the big bold line representing the equator. At the time, I was one of those tourists.

I meandered around the campus, which included a museum and a gift shop with a stamp allowing you to stamp your passport, if you so chose, to prove you were there. Although I did believe this was not legal to do, I proceeded in the task.

I noticed a building off to the side of the monument and decided to give the knob a turn. The door opened. The room was darkly lit, and shelves held Incan relics. In the middle of the room was a table about 4' x 4' with a map.

I walked around the map on the table. Quito was placed in the middle with lines drawn projecting in different directions. They seemed random, yet the angles seemed consistent. The northernmost part of the map was México D.F., the southernmost was mid-Argentina.

What happened next was possibly the most fantastic thing I learned on this entire trip.

The earth rotated in space angled at 23.5 degrees. This gave us the seasons in the different hemispheres. We all learned that in science class back in the day.

When you looked at a piece of Incan art, such as a rug, for example, you would see a consistent pattern at an angle. That angle was approximately 23.5 degrees. So did the Inca know what angle our big blue planet sat at in the universe?

Think about this, in Chichén Itzá, the Temple of Kukulcán (Mayan for "feathered serpent") was a four-sided pyramid. The temple had 91 steps on each side with the final platform on top totaling 365 steps, which equaled the number of days in the year. Because of its design and precise location, on the spring and fall equinoxes the sun hits the temple and casts a shadow, giving the illusion of a serpent slithering down the temple.

So could the Inca have known the angle at which the earth sat in space? Moving around the map, lines were drawn, interestingly from where the actual Mitad del Mundo was.

Actual? Wasn't I at the actual Mitad del Mundo? I mean, there was a big stripe painted outside representing the equator, a gift shop, touristy things.

It turned out the Inca nailed it.

Not too far away, found by the use of GPS, was Catequilla. Catequilla in Quechua means "follower of the moon." At Catequilla was a semicircle wall, and at the center of the circle was the Mitad del Mundo. At one end was the equator. The two ends of the wall, it so happened, created a 23.5-degree angle with one end of the wall aligning with the rising sun of the winter solstice and the other end aligning with the setting sun of the summer solstice.

From that point, Catequilla was placed on the map that I was staring at, and from there, more lines were drawn. One line along the equator, and another perpendicular to the equator at Catequilla. From there, lines drawn at 23.5 degrees extended straight to Quito, Machu Picchu, Chichén Itzá, and Washington DC, which was laid out, some say, by the Masons.

The whole experience was amazing. My mind was buzzing. Although I was seeing this play out, I simply couldn't grasp the complexity of it all.

To go one step further, when the Spanish arrived in Quito, they built churches over the heathen Inca structures, which all aligned with the solstice. In December, the sun penetrated the cupola of the Church of San Francisco, which strikes a triangle above the altar. As the day progresses, the light moves down and creates a glow on the face of the image entitled "God the Father." This happens on the winter solstice.

Mind… Blown.

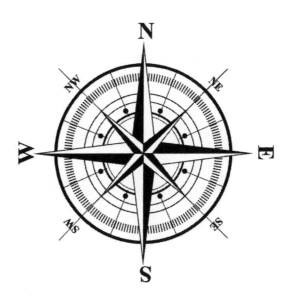

BACK IN QUITO

I found a black market to buy a new pair of running shoes. Adidas knockoffs for ten dollars. I then went for a thirty-minute run, climbed a few hundred stairs to start my training, and played fútbol with some kids in an alley before heading back to my sterile hostel on the empty university campus.

I decided to leave for Riobamba in the morning just three and a half hours south of Quito, which would take me along "The Avenue of Volcanoes."

I read about an epic train ride that seemed like a good way to see a little more of the countryside and have a new experience.

The city of Quito is surrounded by six volcanoes:

Name	Type	Last Eruption
Volcán Cotacachi	Dormant	950 BC
Volcán Pichincha	Stratovolcano	2002
Volcán Cayambe	Complex	1786
Volcán Antisana	Stratovolcano	1802
Volcán Sincholagua	Stratovolcano	Pleistocene era
Cotopaxi	Stratovolcano	2016

We passed Cotopaxi with its impressive stature, rising 19,340' and piercing the dark blue sky with its snowcapped peak. Even before the Inca conquered the Quechua, they considered Cotopaxi a sacred mountain, home to the gods.

The land was rolling and full of farming, along with smatterings of beaten-down restaurants, homes, vendors, mercados, and shelters dotting the landscape. Buses didn't travel fast in Ecuador, but depending on what you were willing to spend, they could be clean and comfortable.

Just after the city of Ambato to the west was Volcán Chimborazo, last eruption 550 AD.

When I was in my teens, we went to the big island of Hawaii to visit some friends of my parents. It was an eye-opening experience in so many ways. First was the size of the plane. I had flown almost exclusively on DC-9s. This was a DC-10. It could hold up to 380 passengers, twice that of a DC-9, and had three rows across and sections, each with its own movie screen. On one trip to Hawaii, my little brother got lost coming back from the lavatory.

"Attention passengers, we have a lost blue-eyed, blond-haired boy looking for his parents." You could hear him crying in the background.

Second was flying over an ocean. This was a bit intimidating the first time. Looking out from thirty thousand feet and seeing only clouds and ocean was surreal when it was your first time. I mean if you had engine problems up here, there was no emergency landing strip. At this point, one put a lot of faith in the pilots and the engineers.

No matter how expensive the equipment, it always comes down to a five-cent washer and a twenty-seven-cent bolt to hold an engine on.

Among the many things I learned while in Hawaii, was that Mauna Kea was actually the tallest mountain in the world when measured from base to peak. Its base was at the bottom of the ocean and put Mauna Kea at 33,500'. Everest was the highest altitude above sea level at 29,029'.

The top of Volcán Chimborazo however was not the highest or the tallest, but it was the furthest point from the center of the earth and the closest point on the earth to space, beating out Everest by 1.5 miles, because of earth's centrifugal bulge.[29]

Oh, and just in case you were wondering, the shortest mountain in the world was Mount Wycheproof, standing proudly at 141' in Wycheproof, Australia.

---

29 The centrifugal bulge is created due to the centrifugal force of the earth spinning in space, making the earth actually an oval, not a sphere.

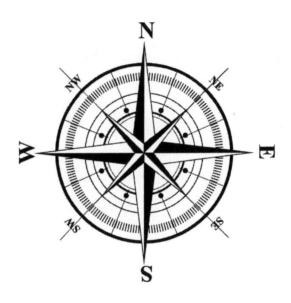

RIOBAMBA

"River Plain"

Arriving just after 11:30 a.m., I found La Mansión Santa Isabella, a run-down Spanish Colonial building.

I was amazed at the tremendous attention to architectural detail that went into all these buildings, the colors, the accents. Sadly, most of these hundreds-of-years-old buildings haven't had the opportunity of continuous maintenance. I still marveled at the detail put into everything from the ornate millwork of the check-in counter to the elaborate door hinges. I suppose with forced labor, in this case the Spanish used the indigenous people, one could build cities and erect grand cathedrals to the God the Spanish introduced to the conquered people.

The woman who checked me in was from Slovakia. She had been in Riobamba for about a month, earning money working at the Mansión for a free room and money so she could continue traveling.

"How much for a room?"

"For how many hours?"

I was confused by the question. "Hours? I don't know. I would like to stay the night."

"Okay. Eight dollars." She wrote my passport number down, standard procedure, and gave me the key. "Upstairs, the room above us. Room siete. Um, seven."

"Thank you. Do you happen to know where the nearest ATM is?"

"Banco Pichincha is just around the corner."

"What's going on?" A rather important-looking parade was going on just outside.

"Some sort of religious event."

The street outside was chock-full of people and a long procession of odd costumes—odd costumes that were dancing and walking and twirling.

The stairs and floors all creaked when I walked to my room. The walls were cracked from centuries of settling and lack of attention. The bed sagged. There was a small wooden table and chair and a small balcony that overlooked Av. José Veloz, which was abundantly busy along the cobblestone street, now packed with thousands celebrating El Pase del Niño.

The shared bathroom was down the hall.

El Pase del Niño celebration was a mixture of the imported Catholic religion combined with Andean ancestral mythology and Pagan traditions. Like voodoo with its marriage of Catholicism and traditional religions of West Africa, these celebrations and beliefs became muddy yet wondrous and curious and mystical.

As I was sitting on the corner watching the parade, a young Ecuadorian sat next to me.

"Excuse me, do you speak English?" he asked.

"Yes." I had no interest in engaging.

"I am a student and am studying English. I would like to pay you to teach me English."

"I'm not really a teacher. I wouldn't know where to begin."

"I would just like to have conversation, practice English. Is that okay? We can go to your hotel."

I had heard of the many scams one might come across in South America. I didn't blame them really. I mean, they were just trying to make money. They had nothing, well nothing in relation to most backpackers. I mean if you had the means to travel internationally, no matter the shoestring budget, you were clearly better off than many of the occupants of the country you were visiting.

The scam that was being set up now was: he convinces me to go to my room, his friends follow in the shadows, and once in the room, they jump me and steal everything.

"I can talk to you here if you want to practice English."

He really pressed going back to my room. I finally just ignored him and after about five minutes he stood up.

He looked at me and said, "¡Pendejo!" Then walked away.

Pfft, pendejo, I've been called worse, I thought.

> "IT AIN'T WHAT THEY CALL YOU, IT'S WHAT YOU
> ANSWER TO."
> – *W.C. Fields.*

By South American standards, I was off to bed early.

For the first time since I left Minneapolis, and still without a watch, I could accurately tell the time in the morning and evening. Here at the equator, the sun rises about six a.m. and sets around six p.m. every day of the year, give or take a few minutes. No need to impress you, the reader, with my sun wizardry.

Back in the room, perhaps thirty minutes later, when I realized something unusual about the Mansión Santa Isabella. There was an unusual amount of foot traffic inside the mansion. Doors were constantly opening and shutting. I could hear couples giggling as they walked up and then later back down the creaky floors to their rooms. The walls were thin, and the sounds of sex could be heard through the cracked walls. It was college dorms all over again.

Now I understood why the Slovakian receptionist asked how many hours I wanted the room. The rooms were rented out by the hour for the sole purpose of sex. These hotels were called "sex hotels."

People have sex. It's no big secret. It's an urge that is sometimes greater than hunger, especially as a horny teenager or twenty-something. Oh, who am I kidding, at any age.

In South America, life was a tad different. People usually didn't move out of their parent's house until they were married. So if you wanted to have sex, you were going to need a place.

These hotels provided the perfect solution for those concerned about having a good reputation. Everyone knew everyone else was having sex, but no one really talked about it.

Where were philandering husbands supposed to take their mis-
tresses? They couldn't just take them home, now could they?

It didn't take long to realize the whole "Latino lover" was an
exaggeration. Pay for an hour to last just two-to-three minutes. Poor
girl. Apparently, foreplay wasn't a Latino thing.

At the bus station, I ran into a couple of backpackers coming back from the Devil's Nose Train ride, which was the whole
point of me coming here. They informed me the train only runs
two days a week, and the next time it departed was in five days.
Disappointing news to say the least. The trip to Riobamba wasn't
an entire waste. I got to see a little of Riobamba, drive along the
"Avenue of Volcanoes," experience a "love hotel," and El Pase del
Niño celebration.

BACK IN QUITO

I found a livelier hostel. It was Christmas Eve. My new roommates were: two Aussies, three Brits, two other US Americans—brother and sister, Ross and Rachel. Finally, there was another English woman with her newly acquired Quechua boyfriend. The pair had just returned from the Amazon, and she was recovering from some jungle ailment. She was horribly ill and covered in hickies, which she was more than eager to show. The hickies were scattered around her body, given to her by the elder women of the jungle community who attempted to "suck" the evil (illness) out of her. Did it work? Well, she was still sick and the ayahuasca journey didn't seem to heal her.

Christmas Eve in Quito

The hostel owner brought a couple of us some gifts: cocaine and weed. We, in turn, supplied alcohol: bottles of vodka, Jameson, Glenlivet, and several bottles of wine, along with more mind-altering substances for the present group.

The hostel owner locked the doors and turned up the music. Manu Chao was his preferred music for the evening, with a few Christmas songs. I believe "Fairytale of New York" by The Pogues was played no less than four times, each time we drunkenly sang arm in arm:

"It was Christmas Eve babe

In the drunk tank

An old man said to me, won't see another one

And then he sang a song

The Rare Old Mountain Dew

I turned my face away

And dreamed about you"

We danced the night away in a sort of fantastic drug-and-alcohol induced haze. I'd love to be able to tell you more about the evening, but all I could tell you for sure was I woke up to the sound of sex coming from the bunk below me. Santa brought your hero a hangover.

MERRY CHRISTMAS 2001

Around 10:00 am, we gathered in the lobby of the hostel. It was decided the night before that we would treat ourselves to the Christmas buffet at the Hilton to celebrate the holiday.

The topic of conversation was sharing what our memorable family traditions were.

After the buffet, we all returned to the hostel and napped. The next day, many left to new destinations and adventures. We stayed in touch via email. It just so happened that ten years later, Rachel emailed me to tell me she ran into the Australian guy at a coffee shop in Santiago, Chile.

I had wanted to go to the Galápagos and do some diving; however, after spending $2800 for the Antarctica adventure, I decided to be frugal and vow to return. The Galápagos and wildlife would be there if the Chinese didn't poach all the wildlife first.[30]

I headed out for a run. Rachel asked to join, and we ran through and around Parque La Carolina. Paved trails weaved through the 165-acre park in the middle of Quito. We ran past a water park, the botanical and Japanese gardens, and along the boulevard of the flowers that opened up into a giant green field surrounded by a running track guarded by a statue of Ecuador's only Olympic medalist,

---

30 In 2020, the Chilean Navy intercepted the Chinese fishing vessels who were illegally fishing in Galápagos waters.

Jefferson Pérez. He took gold for racewalking in Atlanta in 1996 and then won the silver in Beijing in 2008.

Continuing north, off to the left of the trail, a tad bit out of place, a DC-6 airplane, artistically graffitied, sat on a concrete slab. An odd thing to see in such a wonderful park.

I asked back at the hostel about its significance. The hostel owner didn't even know there was a DC-6 covered with graffiti in the park.

Reaching the end of the park at Avenida Naciones Unidas, we ran east and then back south on different trails to see more of the park. The three-mile run was not too bad considering we were at 9300' in elevation.

During our run, we hatched a plan. Her brother Ross and the two of us would hightail it to Cusco, Perú, for New Years. We heard it was quite a celebration. I had also learned that Robin and Nicki, who I met in México and traveled a little around Guatemala with, would be there. It was just one small objective inside one greater one.

Ormeño bus lines boasted having the longest bus route in the world. Over 3,850 miles, you could travel from Lima, Perú, to Rio de Janeiro, Brazil, [at the time of my trip].

So when I bought my ticket from Quito to Tumbes, Perú, you'd have thought the company that boasted the longest bus route in the world would have change for five dollars.

"Keep the change," I conceded to the woman selling me my ticket. She was a bit flustered by the gesture. I don't think people did that, but it was like $0.75 she owed me, and I didn't want to wait around while she found someone with actual change.

Bus to Perú

Rachel, Ross, and I gathered our rucksacks along with Ross's guitar and headed out to the bus estación for a night bus to Tumbes. It would be roughly a fourteen-hour bus ride.

The road took us back through the Avenue of Volcanoes, stopping in Riobamba. The waning gibbous moon shed a gentle light over the spine of Ecuador's Andean range.

We stopped in Riobamba for about thirty minutes to unload and load passengers, stretch the legs, and seek out refreshments and snacks peddled by the dozens of Quechua women. I asked the bus driver the time. He said una y media (1:30).

From Riobamba to La Troncal, we dropped over 12,800' in elevation over a distance of one hundred miles. For the time being, the Andes were behind us, and Ecuador's humid coastal flat lands spread around us as far as you could see. Palm trees and fruit crops hugged the road. The windows were wet with dew from the humidity. The sun was just rising as we reached Naranjal. By the time we reached immigration in Huaquillas, it was close to noon, if I were to guess. Time didn't matter anymore. It hadn't mattered for almost four months. Aside from bus and airplane departure times, time didn't exist.

The whole scene was overwhelming, warm, and humid. Smells of amazing foods and urine intertwined with the lingering smell of fires that seemed to just constantly burn. Garbage lined the streets as hundreds of vendors sold fruits, vegetables, meat, clothes, and an assortment of trinkets and household wares.

We walked the crowded street, and as the only gringos on the bus, it was pretty obvious with the large backpacks, blond hair, and Ross's guitar that we weren't from around here. With that came the unwanted swarm of new "amigos."

Our mission was to get across the border and then off to Tumbes, Perú, where we would figure out our next steps.

Immigration in Ecuador was quick and without any hassle, made slightly easier when one of the passengers showed us where the immigration office was, as it was not at all obvious.

I still had plenty of time on my visa and they required no departure tax from US Americans. Getting the Perú stamp was a bit more of a head scratcher. You'd think that next to Ecuador immigration, there would then be the Perúvian immigration office, stamps stamped, and off you'd go.

Not here, not at this "la frontera." There was no fence, no police, no border control, no indication of any sense of order.

We just stood there with our passports in some sort of no-man's land. We had no stamp in our passport that would prove we were here or there or anywhere.

When buying the ticket, it was either made clear and I didn't understand her, or it wasn't made clear and I simply assumed when buying our bus tickets that once at the Ecuadorian border, the bus stops, we disembark in an orderly manner, and wait in line. Then we'd be directed to the Perúvian immigration, reload the bus and it'd be all wine and roses.

Apparently, the bus didn't even cross the border, and aside from having no clue what to do next, we had to find transport to continue to Tumbes. I didn't know if I was upset or amused. It was midday. We stuck out for sure. Three tall blond people with backpacks and a guitar with a look of wonderment in our eyes and confusion on our faces.

An old man passed us, struggling to push a wheelbarrow full of pineapples up a small incline. Ross and I helped him to his final destination, a hundred feet down the road.

A beer sounded good right about now, as did an empanada. While looking for where I might acquire such a wonderful meal, a man approached us with purpose.

"Amigos, I can take you across the border. Inmigración policía is almost two kilometers away."

We looked at each other waiting for one of us to make a decision. We all stood indifferent. I spotted a vendor with empanadas.

"It's very hot. I charge only ten dollars."

"Ten dollars! Our bus ride from Quito was less than five dollars. How about three dollars? One dollar for each of us."

"You have lots of bags…"

"Okay five dollars." I assumed he didn't have change.

"Okay, five dollars. My car is here. Vamos."

His car was an old station wagon, and in just a few minutes, he dropped us off at Control de Migraciones in Zarumilla, Perú.

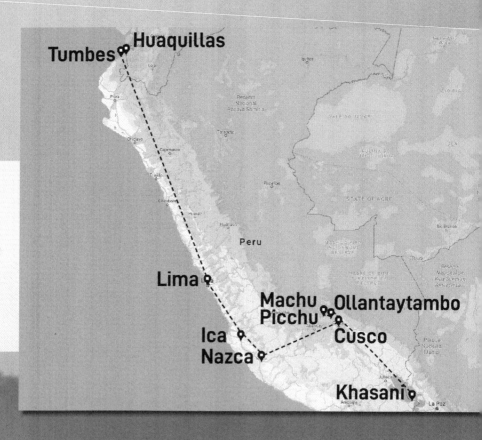

REPUBLIC OF PERÚ

REPUBLIC OF PERÚ

"Derived from Biru, a Sixteenth-Century Leader"

With proof, we were now somewhere, thanks to the stamps fresh in our passports. A colectivo driver waved us over.

"¿Tumbes?"

"Sí."

"Diez soles per persona."

Ten soles, shit how much is that? We hadn't exchanged our USD yet, although it wasn't that the opportunity was lacking with all the money exchangers.

The nice thing about Ecuador, for me selfishly, was they had recently done away with their last currency, the sucre, and replaced it with the US dollar.

Ecuador had gone through epic inflation because of President Abdalá Bucaram, aka El Loco Que Ama, "The Madman Who Loves." He stole a few million dollars' worth of sucre, doing a bit of damage to the economy of Ecuador by crushing the sucre's value. In 2000, President Jamil Mahuad announced the dollarization of the economy of Ecuador, and ever since, the US dollar has been Ecuador's official currency.

I think I saw that one dollar would get you about 3.60 solas.

Now in Perú, I was back to math. Converting dollars into Perúvian sol.

With that, there was a new experience I would soon come across. The world of counterfeiters. What experience did we helpless backpackers have in what a real sol was versus a counterfeit one? They preyed on us gringos.

Urban legend claimed that the word gringo stemmed from when the United States invaded México in 1846. Wearing green uniforms, the Mexican people yelled: "Green Go Home!"

In fact, the word comes from the Greek word *griego*, which means Greek, which sort of means, it's all Greek to me. So any foreigner speaking a language that is not understood is a gringo.

We found an old man sitting in a fold-up chair, dressed in a dirty and dated tweed suit and a sun-beaten fedora. His chair sat in a patch of dirt off the side of the road. On his lap was an open briefcase full of Perúvian sols, US dollars, and various other currencies from around the world. The euro didn't start going to print for another five days, Jan. 1, 2002. I didn't really like the idea of the euro for nostalgic reasons. I liked all my German, Swiss, Austrian, Dutch, and French coins.

I paid the colectivo guy thirty soles, and we were off to Tumbes, a half-hour ride even farther south. I really wanted an empanada.

Tumbes

Tumbes, Tumbes, Tumbes. If you asked me what to do in Tumbes, I would say leave. That was really not fair actually. I didn't even give it a chance, but from what I saw, it wasn't captivating.

The upside of traveling with Ross and Rachel was they were open to last-minute changes, which was fine since we knew we wanted to be in Cusco by New Years. How that happened was how it happened.

Four flights were scheduled from Tumbes to Lima for fifty USD. The one-hour-thirty-minute flight would put us in Lima by six p.m.

The flight saved us time for sure, but it meant we would skip quite a bit of what Perú had to offer. The longer you stayed anywhere, the longer you realized the amount of things there were to see and do. Taste and smell. Love and hate or be completely indifferent about.

One place, of the many places that we would miss, which was of particular interest to me, was the Chan Chan ruins of the Chimú people. The Chimú were considered to be the most advanced civilization in Perú before the Inca conquered them in 1470.

Lima

Aeropuerto Internacional Pedro Canga Rodríguez was a large open-air rectangle room. Security was one guy with a machine gun. No metal detectors, no x-ray—a world of difference compared to my recent experiences in Panama and Venezuela. A single runway hosted a sun-beaten DC-9. Aeropuerto Internacional Jorge Chávez was not as simple, but considering it was an international hub, it certainly lacked complexity.

In the main entrance/exit lobby, a replica of a Chávez's Blériot XI airplane caught my eye. It hung from the ceiling, wedged between the wall and a large column, sort of placed there as an afterthought. Like the architect said while doing the punch list, "Oh shit, that's right. The client wanted us to hang a Blériot XI airplane from the ceiling... this will do."

Jorge, for whom the airport was named, flew higher than any other pilot back in 1910, exceeding 8500'. His biggest claim to fame was being the first person to fly over the Alps successfully, with a catch. While the flight was successful, during landing, the wings broke off on his Blériot XI, and he and his plane fell over 60'. He died four days later from his injuries at the age of twenty-three.

Our next tasks were as follows:

1. Hire taxi

2. Check into hostel

3. Find "black" market

Ross stayed back at the hostel to play his guitar or meet new people. He was extremely engaging.

Rachel and I took a taxi down to one of Lima's "black markets" to acquire a couple of new music CDs and stop at a farmacia to pick up some Valium or similar medicine, as I hadn't been sleeping. Our driver took us to what appeared to be the shadiest part of Lima. It looked as if a war had just ended. Garbage was everywhere, homelessness was rampant, the sounds of music overlapped, food sizzled. Autos, mopeds, and tuk-tuks honked their horns incessantly. A tent city crammed into a chain-link fence controlled by no one, filled with everything, running independently from the world outside the fence.

Steam from cauldrons and grills emitted a variety of smells, women nursed their babies and cooked, children sat, dirty-looking and tired. I purchased some beef heart from a vendor. It was quite tasty, and I washed it down with a couple of Cusqueña cervezas. It was late, ten p.m., when we headed back to our hostel. I knew this because after four months of traveling, I had finally bought a watch.

December 28, we jumped on a bus to Ica. We heard it was where one goes if one wanted to sandboard on sand dunes. It would be four and a half hours before we arrived in Ica. The person who sat next to me was a twenty-something-year-old Perúvian woman who was VERY friendly. Her name was Kari. She spoke bueno English and was headed to Santiago, Chile, for a vacation.

"Santiago, I'll be going there in a month or so. Don't know when exactly. I want to visit the Concha y Toro vineyard."

She grabbed my arm tightly, looked around with wide eyes, and put her finger over her month. "Shhhhh. Don't say that word."

"What word?"

"Concha," she whispered.

"Concha?" I replied in my normal voice. "It's the name of the vineyard? Concha y Toro. Doesn't it mean shell and bull. Not really sure of the connection between the two."

She covered her face embarrassed. "NO, concha means," she pointed to her crotch, "vagina."

Actually, it was a bit more vulgar when used as an insult. For example, "¡Tu madre es una concha!" translates to "Your mother is a c*&t."

Just one border crossing away and the name of the largest vineyard in South America took on a whole new meaning.

During our flirtatious engagement, she asked to look at the stamps in my passport. I grabbed my passport, along with all my cash and soon-to-be non-working debit card. She went through each page and touched each stamp as if by doing so it allowed her to experience the country.

The way things were going, I was surprised she hadn't asked me to come home with her to meet her parents. My guess was she had our wedding already planned. She was an aggressive pursuer for sure.

Ica

Once in Ica, I said goodbye to her and reached for my CamelBak on the shelf above me. It was gone. Stolen, no doubt at one of the many stops along the way. Lifted by one of the passengers who took advantage of the fact that I was engulfed in conversation with Kari.

For those of you who may not have done the backpacker thing: It's common to see backpackers wearing their big pack on their back and a small day pack, or in my case, the CamelBak, the one I just bought in Boulder, in the front.

Ninety-nine percent of the time, when I got on a bus, I sat hugging my CamelBak or had it tied or fastened to my leg in some way to inform me, like a fish bobber, if someone was attempting to steal it or rifle through it.

Today, for whatever reason, I decided to put this pack on the above storage shelf. Just a stupid move.

My CD player and collection of bootlegged CDs were gone along with my camera that "embodied all the latest technology."[31] Had I not removed my passport, cash, and debit card, this story would have taken a completely different trajectory.

The facts were these:

Fact 1:   My CamelBak was gone along with the contents.

Fact 2:   There was nothing I could do about it.

Fact 3:   There were sand dunes to descend.

As we collected our bags, Kari stood behind me and collected her suitcase.

"What are you doing? I thought you were going to Santiago."

"I want to stay with you."

"But you're going on vacation? I am just here for the day and

31 TBATB

then heading to Cusco for New Year's. You should continue on to your vacation."

"This is like vacation."

"I'm not going to tell you what to do, but our plans are pretty loose. We might not even stay the night here. We want to go to Nazca before Cusco."

"That's okay, I want to be with you now."

She smiled, and we were now four. A taxi took us to Oásis de la Laguna Huacachina where we exchanged a few soles for a piece of plywood cut in the shape of a snowboard with two Velcro straps attached to it to serve as bindings. Didn't get much for the money, but then again, I didn't expect much.

Not a chance in hell these Velcro "bindings" would hold your feet in place, but that was what made the event so damn entertaining. All you could do was start your descent and then when the Velcro gave out, you just tumbled down the dune at great speeds. Sand found its way in every crack and crevice of the human body. After four times up and down, it was time for a couple of beers. While sitting on a chair with my head back, taking in the sun, Kari started giving me a foot massage. While reader, it was true I did not turn down the massage, this "relationship" was becoming awkward.

Ross, Rachel, and I jumped in the "Oasis of America" in an attempt to rid ourselves of sand and dirt. Then the four of us took a taxi back to town to arrange a bus to Nazca.

Kari suddenly changed her mind and decided to continue on to Santiago. Or so she said. She gave me a kiss and her phone number for when I got back to Lima. Returning to Lima wasn't on my radar, but then again, it wasn't not on my radar.

Then the news we didn't expect to hear. All the buses to Nazca were booked. Our game plan needed to be reworked. So we sat in the Plaza de Armas thinking about options.

Two Perúvian officers were walking the plaza. For reasons still unknown, perhaps a subconscious response to my CamelBak being stolen, I decided to approach the two officers and asked if they would sell me one of their police badges.

One officer laughed, but the other one wanted to know how much I would pay.

"Ten USD," I answered.

He thought for a moment. "Perhaps twenty."

"Done." I assumed he would just take the badge off his hat and sell it to me on the spot.

Instead, he walked me over to the policía car. Ross and Rachel stayed back. The other officer joined us at the car. We drove to the police station, where the officer who was willing to sell me his badge went inside. I could see him through the window trying to take the badge off another officer's hat. Then I watched as he got caught.

Returning to the car, he informed me it would be impossible. I said, "Thirty dollars." The two officers looked at each other, and we soon found ourselves parked in front of a residence. This happened to be the police chief's house. The chief stood in his lit doorway, listening to the officer. The chief entered his house and then returned, handed the officer something, went back inside, and shut the door. The officer returned and said, "Forty dollars," and handed me the badge.

I paid him the money, and he returned us back to the plaza.

Policía Nacional del Perú—PNP. The motto on the badge read: "Dios, Patria, Ley." ("God, Fatherland, Law.")

A group of young Perúvians watched me being "released" from the back of the policía car. After the police left, they approached me to inquire what was going on. I showed them the badge, and they were in shock. Every one of them offered to buy it from me.

The Perúvian National Police was the largest police force in Latin America. This badge carried the same weight as having an FBI badge.

Realizing there was no way I was going to sell them the badge, we told them our situation. One of the guys said for fifty dollars, he'd drive us in his car to Nazca. We could leave immediately. We agreed to the "taxi," and he disappeared, re-appearing with a friend and a 1970s Dodge Coronet. I checked my watch. It was 10:27 p.m.

As we left town and entered the desert, the following *Blues Brothers* scene came to mind:

Elwood: "There's 106 miles to Chicago, we've got a full tank of gas, half a pack of cigarettes, it's dark out, and we're wearing sunglasses."

Joliet Jake: "Hit it!"

Nazca was 150 km (93 miles) south, about a two-and-a-half-hour drive. A bus ticket would have cost us seven dollars each, but we decided on an acceptable fare, and then there was the experience.

We'd arrive sometime after one a.m., giving us time to find a room, sleep in a little, fly around the Nazca Lines, and board a bus to Cusco. Just in time for New Year's.

Outside of Ica, southbound on the Pan-American Highway, our driver turned off the headlights.

"It saves gas," he said to us, looking at the review mirror with a smile.

It wasn't the first time I've heard or seen this tactic. It could be argued that driving with the headlights off did save on gas. The alternator puts out more current to run the lights, which does in fact increase the work the motor does to run the alternator. The difference in gas mileage was infinitesimal.

The moon was in its waxing gibbous phase, offering plenty of light as it glowed infinitely along the ancient land. It was the "black taxi" that I told myself in Nebraska I would not do again.[32] But here I sat, in the back of this car with two strangers and Ross and Rachel.

About an hour out, the road slowed as it weaved up and over a mountain range just north of Palpa and a second range just south. Thirty minutes after Palpa, we could see the glow of the city of Nazca.

The driver looked back with a smile, pointing to the right toward a vast empty swathe of land, and said, "Líneas de Nazca aquí."

32 TBATB

NAZCA

Like a kid on Christmas morning, I was up at sunrise, champing at the bit to get to the airport. I couldn't wait to see the Nazca Lines. However, we had to wait, so I buttered up some toast, had a fried egg, and drank a couple cups of coffee.

My stomach gurgled. I was a bit gassy. Something wasn't 100 percent, but…Nazca Lines!

I had an unhealthy interest in the paranormal, mysteries of the unknown, aliens, and the like. The Nazca Lines tapped into it all. Telepathy, aliens, ancient astronauts.

Our day consisted of two goals:
1.   Nazca Lines
2.   Bus tickets to Cusco, getting us into Cusco midday on December 31.

The airport in Nazca was designed pretty much for the sole purpose of taking tourists up a couple thousand feet to circle the Nazca Desert and catch a glimpse of these ancient mysterious lines. I bought my ticket along with a couple of disposal cameras.

The pilot flew the Cessna with precision and used the wings to point toward the different geoglyphs.

Roughly eight hundred lines or "runways" laid out, stretching as long as twelve hundred feet. It was astonishing to experience them firsthand. Why were they here? What was their purpose? Who were they built for? I wanted to go back, time travel. Understand, it was all so simple yet so complex. Some say the lines were runways for aliens. Others say they were a religious homage to their gods. Others have hypothesized the lines pointed to underwater sources. The truth is, nobody living today knows. Maybe they are nothing more than just giant doodles.

Geoglyph of a spider. (Shutterstock image)

The pilot circled the flat desert. It appeared empty, then suddenly, like after staring at an autostereogram, images started to appear:

- Hummingbird
- Monkey
- Pelican
- Tree
- Spider
- Condor
- Whale
- Hands

And then there was the Astronaut, a sort of anthropomorphic being, created on the side of a hill, looking to the heavens and waving to the gods.

Ancient astronauts are nothing new. Not that there is 100 percent proof either way, there have certainly been some head-scratching images left around the world. Throughout time, humans have "documented" the potential existence of aliens:

15,000 BC:	Saucer-shaped object	Cave of Pech Merle
12,000 BC:	Cave painting of UFO	Niaux, France
10,000 BC:	"The astronauts"	Valcamonica, Italy
5,000 BC:	Rocket ship cave painting	Japan
776 AD:	Illustration of a crusader sighting a UFO	
1710 AD:	The Baptism of Christ by Aert de Gelder	

After the flight over the Nazca Lines, we found a bus station and learned that every bus to Cusco was sold out. It appeared Cusco was a popular destination for New Year's Eve.

Determined to get there, we found ourselves standing on the dirt shoulder of the Pan-American Highway, thumbs out, in hopes of hitching a ride to Cusco, just 406 miles away.

If ever in Perú, one of the popular delicacies is choclo con queso (corn with cheese). The corn, with its oversized sweet kernels, and the cheese, salty and soft, is an amazing combination. You can find it everywhere being peddled by Quechua children and women through partially open windows on buses. Exact change recommended.

I couldn't get enough of this newfound staple. It wasn't heavy, you never really felt full, but it was satisfying and cheap. That and I loved the salty cheese. Nibble the corn, take a bite from the block of cheese. Repeat. Well, the thing was, the cheese was unpasteurized and with that, one could get a handful of fun bacteria that caused vomiting and diarrhea.

Sitting in the sun, baking in the eighty-degree weather, shit got real, for real.

All that unpasteurized cheese was coming for me in a medieval way. I came down with the worst diarrhea ever experienced by any person in the history of humankind. Fortunately, there was a small family-run restaurant across the Pan-American.

Doing all my best to stop the carnage, I rammed through the café's swinging doors, surprising the family preparing some sort of delicious-smelling food. I didn't have time.

"¡¡¡¡BAÑO!!!! ¿¡¿¡¿¡¿Tiene baño?!?!?!?"

"Sí, sí, sí. ¡Por ahí!" The woman pointed to another set of café swinging doors at the opposite end of the room. They opened into a three-foot by two-foot closet with a squat toilet and offered virtually no privacy. I didn't care.

For those of you who don't know what a squat toilet is, it's essentially a hole in the ground that you squat over if you happen to be taking a shit.

Aside from having abruptly barged into this restaurant, I found myself with my shorts around my ankles, both hands pressed against the walls, watching the family as they watched me... how can I say this politely evacuate into their squatter. The doors were short and high exposing my head from the shoulders up and then my knees down.

The mom made a sign of the cross. The three children looked at me laughing.

I was in a cold sweat. Worse yet—there was no toilet paper. This shit was messy. I had no choice; I had to sacrifice my underwear in the name of sanitation, and I use that word very loosely.

I walked back out to meet Ross and Rachel.

"You made it!" Rachel yelled, laughing.

"Barely. I think I need Imodium."

A taxi pulled up. The driver asked if we needed a ride. He spoke English quite well, and we told him our situation. He thought about it for a while and said that he would return in ten minutes.

Fifteen minutes later, he returned with his two brothers. "We will take you to Cusco. It will be sixty US dollars."

"Are you serious?! You think six of us are going to fit in that car with all our gear? No way."

"Yes, sure, amigo, no problemo. We put mochilas (backpacks) on top with guitar."

It was a four-door hatchback Daewoo Tico. The tyres on this baby were size 135/80R12—I looked out of curiosity.

The distance from Nazca to Cusco was just over four hundred miles. That was the same distance as say:

Amsterdam to Berlin.

New York City to Montréal, Canada.

The countries of Iceland, Hungary, and Portugal are half the size in distance.

Add in a total elevation gain of just over 36,000' if you included all the highs and lows along the way. Mauna Kea had nothing on us.

Backpacks strapped to the top, forty-eight horsepower under the hood, Ross said a little prayer, and vroom, vroom, we were off to champion up and through the Andes.

We stopped frequently to stretch and negotiate road conditions.

It was eighteen hours of driving before our taxi driver decided he didn't want to continue. I had to give him props for going this far. Between the river crossings, sketchy plank bridges, countless miles of dirt roads, and almost one thousand pounds of passenger weight and gear, his little Tico was beat up.

Taxi to Cusco.

That didn't stop me from arguing with him as we paid him to take us to Cusco, not some random intersection with a petrol station.

A colectivo rolled up and dropped off a couple of locals.

"¿¡Cusco?!" Rachel shouted at the driver.

"Sí, sí." He thought for a moment, trying to figure out what the gringo upcharge was. "One hundred soles."

How much was that in USD? Oh who cared. Looking around, what other options did we have?

"Okay guys, it's one hundred soles each."

"No, no, señor, todo. One hundred soles todo."

And that's how we met the most honest man in all of Perú.

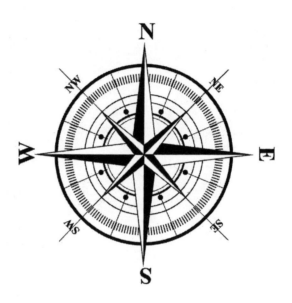

CUSCO

Calle Procuradores off the Plaza de Armas offered hostels and drugs. We walked up the narrow cobblestone street, decorated with graffiti, windows protected by metal grates. Drug dealers perched against the walls, whispering loudly as you walked by, "Weed, you want weed" or "Charlie, charlie."[33]

Checked in to our new hostel, the room was a dark, dank space with four metal spring beds from the early 1900s, supporting a worn-out, stained mattress—possibly also from the early 1900s. I opted to protect myself from any communal diseases the mattress might be hosting by sleeping in my sleeping bag. The fourth bed was occupied by a cheerful Israeli woman by the name of Tali. She was a travel writer for an Israeli travel magazine heading to Machu Picchu in a couple of days. It was decided right then we would all travel together to Machu Picchu.

Leaving Tali to her work, Rachel, Ross, and I walked back to the Plaza de Armas. It was obvious this evening was going to escalate into a heck of a celebration come midnight. Groups of teens gathered with beer and music, the Perúvian flute bands competed over each other, gringos from all over the world were moving targets for the locals to sell over-priced chachkas or taking photos of themselves standing next to Quechuan children with a lamb.

33 Cocaine

A pickpocket's paradise.

Robin and Nicki, who I met in México and traveled with in Guatemala, were here. I decided to find them, agreeing to meet Ross and Rachel in the plaza at four p.m.

I connected with Robin and Nicki. Robin had her boyfriend or fiancé with her. He had flown out for the week from London to spend New Year's with her. They had just returned from Machu Picchu, so we went to celebrate our reunion with a cocktail at a little nameless place near their hostel.

When we entered the bar, there was no one there, not even a bartender. We sat at the bar, reminiscing. Robin told her boyfriend/fiancé about my "Una Vie y Una Vie" story.

"Whatever happened to Gabi?" they asked.

"Last email I got from her was that she met a Russian guy who she couldn't stand, but he had a pickup so she travels for free with him. She will only ride in the back because 'he is so annoying.' She is somewhere in South America."

"What about Paul?"

"Paul's back in Canada."

Still no bartender. I stood up, walked behind the bar, and leaned on the counter. "What do you want?"

"I'll have a martini," Nicki said.

"Oh, I'll have a Pimm's," said Robin.

"A Pimm's?! Nope, you get a martini."

"Make that two," the boyfriend/fiancé chimed in.

Nicki and me at the bar.

It was closing in on four p.m., and I had to meet Ross and Rachel.

"Where do you think we'll run into each other next? London, Hong Kong, Goa?"

The question was left unanswered as we hugged goodbye. The bartender never did show up.

"Cory, got a great idea," Rachel said. "Let's go buy food and hand it out to the homeless."

Looking around the plaza, it was not hard to miss, but easy to ignore, the poor destitute mothers with their dirty-faced children, wrapped in worn-out blankets with a small tray presented to a passerby, hoping to collect change. An arm out, the mothers' sorrow was weaved on their faces.

"Yeah, that is a fantastic idea."

We found the nearest panadería and loaded up with as much bread, rolls, pastries—whatever they had left at the end of the day. We could only carry so much at a time, so we returned again and again until there were no more bread, rolls, or pastries to buy.

When darkness came, the plaza lit up. All cars were removed but one, a regrettable oversight on the owner's part, whose car would be trampled on throughout the night.

First, it started with the occasional bottle rocket, then the bottle rockets became more and more frequent. Children were running around, pan fluters were fluting, music was coming out of every open-air restaurant and bar. The stores were bustling with tourists buying pan flutes, alpaca hats, blankets, coats that they would never wear again, and t-shirts to prove they were here.

The bottle rockets graduated into packs of fireworks snapping. Ground spinning and fountain fireworks went off randomly in the street and in the plaza. I saw a group of kids drinking bottles of wine and asked Rachel to make a photo with me sitting with them.

Me with the kids in the plaza.

Midnight approached, and things became louder, and suddenly, with just a minute to go, like a well-orchestrated dance line, everyone started running around the plaza in a circle. The car received more unwanted trampling. It was a Latin American tradition to run around the plaza, apparently to bring good luck. We joined in and afterward Rachel grabbed me and gave me a kiss.

That was the limit to our physical relationship—some friendships were better that way.

It was now the dawn of 2002, and in all the craziness, Ross informed us his passport and traveler's checks had been stolen. It was not uncommon to have your pocket or backpack slashed by a razor blade, almost unnoticeable when you're packed in a large group. Ross's pocket had been slashed.

The next morning, over breakfast, plans were altered and decisions made. We'd all go to Machu Picchu. Our original plan was to head to Bolivia after that. We discussed smuggling Ross into Bolivia and then finding the US Embassy in La Paz, where he could acquire a new passport. We thought about how immigration had been easy to avoid when we entered Perú. Perhaps the border into Bolivia was equally as uncontrolled. Ross didn't want to risk being turned away at the border and booked a flight to Lima.

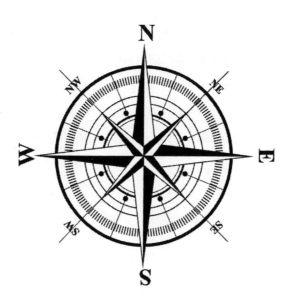

OLLANTAYTAMBO

With our new game plan loosely held together with spit and a prayer, the four of us jumped in a colectivo to the town of Ollantaytambo. We found a cozy cottage-esque, simple stucco building, Spanish tile roof crowned with two ceramic cows. I never noticed this before. I looked around, and it appeared most homes had ceramic cows on top of them.

"¿Qué son esos?" I asked our hostess, who was a short round Quechuan woman with a big smile and a gold front tooth.

"Cómo?"

"Qué son esos?" I asked, pointing at the cows.

"Buena suerte," she responded.

I had no clue what buena suerte meant and figured I never would, but then Ross chimed in.

"She said they were for good luck."

"Dude. You know Spanish?"

"Yeah, pretty fluent."

"WHY have you been letting me struggle for the past few days?"

"How else were you going to learn? You're doing fine." He smiled.

The town was nestled in a flat valley, offering plenty of opportunity for agriculture. The ruins looked down upon the town as ghostly protectors. Trails zigzagged up the steep mountainsides to the tops of the peaks and beyond. Agricultural terraces stepped perfectly up the base of the mountains. Engineering achievement after engineering achievement.

The Templo del Sol was west on the edge of town. The stonework was impossibly precise. The scale and simple complexity of it all was fascinating. Single stones weighing hundreds, if not thousands, of tons somehow cut and moved into place with no tool marks.

Below, just to the southwest, was the Pyramid of Pacaritanpu. This is where I get uncontrollably excited, and to share the reason for my excitement, I would like to introduce you to Brien Foerster, an expert on Inca society, and share his discovery regarding the pyramid.

This intriguing "structure" is rarely if ever shown by guides to Ollantaytambo, mainly because most of them don't even know it is there! And no one, in all of the research that I have done, has a clue who made it or when.

On the winter solstice of each year, June 21, the rays of the rising sun enter and strike the right one of the two windows of the pyramid. This coincides, more or less, with the celebration of the Inti Raymi, which is the Inca celebration of the rebirth of the sun, and of the history of the whole Inca civilization.

According to the Salazars' interpretation of this event and effect, "the sun's light entering this space symbolizes the union between the Sky and the Earth, and the 'illumination' of its heroes is a product of its communion, which is why they were called the Sons of the Sun."

Hence the name "House of the Dawn" has a double meaning, typical of many oral traditions; dawn as in morning, more specifically the morning of the display of the solstice, and dawn as in place and time of origins of a people; the Inca in this case.

Reader, I'll let you take a moment and let that soak in.

Ancient civilizations + masters of astronomy + masters of stone, earth, and water = ancient astronauts? Just tossing it out there.

In the eyes of tourism, and the very reason why we were here, the town now served as a jumping off point to catch the train to Aguas Calientes, the next stop along the way to Machu Picchu.

It also serves as the starting point for those hiking the Inca Trail to Machu Picchu.

Now reader, if you hadn't guessed this already, your hero avoided guided tours as much as possible, and the Inca Trail required a guide. I could not bring myself to hire someone, knowing I am capable of doing the hike self-supported and on my own.

I'm not a snob. I do respect a few of the objections to my objection of hiring a guide.

- Hiring a guide generates economic growth for the community.
- Hiring a guide prevents littering and damage to the ruins.
- Hiring a guide limits the number of people who hike the trail, which helps keep the trails in good repair.

Tali decided to head up the task of buying train tickets. We gave her a little more than what was needed as we didn't have exact change. Standing about five foot two inches, you could tell Tali was a feisty one. Being Israeli, she probably had a few kills under her belt from her mandatory military service.

Undoubtedly, she could survive off dirt and piss, and I was sure she was a master of Krav Maga. So when the woman in the booth selling us the tickets gave her counterfeit money in change, Tali went ballistic.

"¡FALSO! ¡FALSO!" she screamed, pounding the window with her fist and holding up the counterfeit bills with her non-pounding hand at the woman's eye level.

A police officer came over, and soon realized he was no match for a pissed-off former Israeli military soldier who was just handed counterfeit money. A few nods of his head to the woman in the booth, and she exchanged the money for real soles. Just like that, Tali was like, "Cool, let's grab a beer and jump on the train." As if nothing ever happened. I don't even know how she knew it was counterfeit, but she did. We were now on a train—beer in hand.

AGUAS CALIENTES

R iding on the train to Aguas Calientes was exciting. I like trains. I like trams and roller coasters and subways or metros. Where I live, none of these were offered, so being on a train was fun.

In 2000, I flew to Florida and ran the Disney Marathon, then flew to Panama City, Panama. From there, I spent a month wandering around Central America finishing in Cancún. Then, I flew to New Orleans and ran the Mardi Gras Marathon. I then took the Amtrak for three days from New Orleans to Minneapolis by way of Chicago. And you know what? I loved it.

What I didn't love, or perhaps it just really spooked me, was when we arrived in Aguas Calientes and disembarked the train.

Standing on the platform, somehow knowing I was on this train, perhaps by the use of some sort of witchcraft, was Kari, the Perúvian woman who I thought was on her way to Santiago.

Ross and Rachel looked at me, sucked in their lower lips, and widened their eyes as if to say, "Oh boy, good luck with that." With a smirk, Ross said, "Yeah, okay, so we'll just meet you at the hostel."

Tali had no clue what was going on and was not one to involve herself in someone else's business. She just waved at me and went off with Ross and Rachel.

"Sooo, Santiago is a no go?"

"I had to see you again. I have been here for two days. What has taken you so long?" She almost seemed angry.

"What took me so... how did you get here so fast? All the buses were sold out, and I saw you leave south on the bus."

"I flew from Arequipa. It is only less than one hour flight."

Huh, why didn't we think of that? I suppose it seemed counterintuitive to continue on the bus heading further away from our destination, but it would have saved us a day or, according to Kari, two days.

"So, do you want to maybe grab a beer?" She smiled and held my hand. "I am staying at a hostel nearby. You will stay with me tonight?"

Now normally I would jump at the chance for a little frisky business, but at this point, I was so weirded out by her being here, I didn't think I would have had any fun.

I had to dig deep to remember how I escaped uncomfortable encounters in the past. Usually, I had my own car so escape was easy, but here I was trapped in a town where the only mode of escape was a scheduled train. The town wasn't that big, and she clearly had the grit and staying power to starve me out. Besides, her black magic would have found me. I didn't stand a chance.

I ripped the Band-Aid off with a poorly developed story.

"Do you remember Rachel? Well, she and I decided to start a relationship after you left."

"No, I don't believe it. Her boyfriend is Ross. I can see this."

"No, Ross is her brother. The woman that was with us on the train, she is Ross's girlfriend. She met us in Cusco."

What a web I was weaving, but after racking up a bit of a bar tab, she either finally believed me or simply conceded.

She left me with the tab, and I left her with a broken heart.

I gave the group the CliffsNotes version of what I told her. Rachel gave me a big hug and a kiss on the cheek.

"Don't mean to cockblock ya," she said.

"That was the right play," I said.

That night Tali, Ross, Rachel, and I climbed into our individual beds in our shared room and shut out the lights. Tali broke the dark silence with a question. "Have you guys ever done a Dream Walk?"

Ross, Rachel and I all replied with a "No."

Tali then told us she was going to lead us on one, "O.k. Let's do this," she said, and instructed us to lie flat on our backs and close our eyes. Then she began: "Imagine you are walking on a path in the woods. What does the path look like? What do the woods look like? You come to a stream and cross it. What does the stream look like? How did you cross it?"

This went on for about ten minutes. Afterward, Tali told us that each of our answers represented significant things in our lives and how we perceived those things. Then we shared our Dream Walks.

I went last.

When I finished, everyone was silent for a long minute until Rachel chuckled and said, "Dude, that's pretty psychedelic, did you used to take a lot of drugs?"

MACHU PICCHU

"Ancient Mountain"

We were up early, and it was still dark. The trail head up to the top was just over a mile away. It was around fifty degrees Fahrenheit and would only reach perhaps seventy at today's apex.

The climb up through the jungle was steep as we pressed up the ancient staircase. Hundreds of years ago, Inca found, cut, and shouldered these massive steps into place along the steep mountainside. To complain about the ascent would be an insult.

The top reached and entranced gained, we found ourselves amongst a few others who had reached the Guardhouse, which was one of the well-established structures on the site and the recommended viewpoint for sunrise. It was a bit cloudy but, really, I was sitting at one of the most epic ancestral locations in the world. A few clouds weren't going to dampen my mood. They added to the mystique.

Terraces, towers, walls, and doorways with no sense of rhyme or reason held together with no mortar, just perfectly cut stones. And amongst them, llamas grazed in the pastures while tour groups followed their leader, who carried flags.

The scale was fantastic. The whole estate rested in a saddle that was overlooked by Huayna Picchu. Home to the high priest and his collection of virgins, or so sayeth the legend.

What can I say that hasn't been said of Machu Picchu. Epic stonework. Engineering designed to embrace earthquakes. I'm not going to say it… just not going… okay, ancient astronauts?

Climbing to the top of Huayna Picchu was a onetime must for your hero who enjoys *l'appel du vide*. I would be lying if I told you I wasn't petrified as I reached the top and descended back down, but the view was monumental.

I could go on about the site, but as your guide of this story, I will encourage you, if you have not yet been, to have your own Machu Picchu experience.

Our exploration came to an end six hours later. The monumental views over, we began to descend the same ancient stairway.

There were thirteen switchbacks up and down the Carreterra Hiram Bingham road that took thousands of tourists from Aguas Calientes to Machu Picchu and back daily by bus. The road snaked up the side of a steep mountain and cut through the Inca staircase that we opted to ascend and descend.

I came across a young boy who was running down the stairs to meet the tourist buses at each bend. I decided to join him. You could see the older passengers in awe as they came around each switchback to see me and the boy standing there waving.

We returned to our hostel in Aguas Calientes, grabbed our packs, and headed to the train station.

The train back to Cusco should have been time for reflection on where we had just been, humbled by such an important ancient location; instead, we bumped into a couple of rowdy Australians who I immediately warmed up to.

"Mate, let's climb outside the train and ride on the roof."

They weren't asking us. They were in the process of climbing out the window and were TELLING us to join them. Tali was third, then I followed.

So to answer the question asked by my parents, teachers, and authority figures for decades, "If everyone jumped off a bridge, would you?" We now know my answer.

BACK IN CUSCO

One more night in Cusco, we walked around Plaza de Armas one last time, searching for where we might enjoy our last supper.

After hearing about my acquisition of the Perúvian police badge, my uncle Johnny—an avid hat collector—emailed me asking if I could get him a Perúvian police hat.

Two police officers oversaw the plaza, and I approached them.

Along the lines of "if you don't ask, you don't get," I asked the officers if they would sell me their cap with the badge. One walked away, the other took fifty soles and asked me to give him my name and hostel.

Worst case, I was going to be out fifty soles.

After dinner, I decided to buy some patches to repair my back-pack at one of the many stores catering to gringos. A large bowl filled with patches of flags from all over the world sat on a table next to alpaca sweaters.

Huh, maybe I'll get one for each country I've been to and stitch them on my pack.

"How much is a flag?"

"Three American dollars."

"Three dollars?" That seemed high. I had just dropped fifty soles on a hat I might not ever get.

"Okay, my friend. Three for ten dollars."

"Three for ten dollars, how is that a good deal? How about four for ten dollars?"

I bought a total of thirteen and wouldn't sew Bolivia, Chile, or Argentina on until I got there.

Back at the hostel, on the counter was a package wrapped carefully in brown paper tied with a string to Sr. Mortensen. In it was a Perúvian police hat with badge.

On the left, the note from the police officer who sold the hat.
On the right, my new amigo and me showing off our police hats.

Ross headed back to Lima to get a new passport. Tali went south to Arequipa, and Rachel and I headed to Copacabana. It would be over ten hours in a bus before we arrived in Copacabana. I grabbed a book from the "take one, leave one" shelf.

Lost Horizon by James Hilton.

RIDE TO COPACABANA

The bus was fine, though cramped and full of stinky backpackers and stinky locals. But had I known there was a train, I would have paid top dollar for that experience.

I was lost in my new book. It connected with my current journey, slightly different, slightly the same. An adventure that turned into more.

From Cusco, the first 109 miles took us up to an elevation of 14,222', where the region of Cusco ended, the region of Puno began, and the bus stopped for a short break, perhaps a ruse to get us to buy from the fifteen or so Quechua women selling alpaca jackets, sweaters, blankets, ponchos, rugs, and hats. A few unshaven alpacas wandered the plains, brought there for the sake of the tourist.

"Okay, here comes a bus, release the alpacas!" the Quechua women would shout to each other as the bus's hydraulic brakes hissed to a stop.

I really wanted some water as I had drunk my Nalgene dry.

The Nalgene bottle was sort of a trophy case many backpackers cherished. Stickers were how one could show off how much they'd traveled without saying a word. "Oh, I see you've been to Rio de Janeiro." The sticker on the Nalgene told me this without having to engage.

We pulled into Puno late in the night or early in the morning. My watch stopped working and apparently the idea was that we all just sleep on the bus for a couple hours without the option of getting off.

At this point, I didn't bother asking questions about why this or that happened. You just sort of had to know things would work out. It was better to enjoy the experience and appreciate how good you had it where you came from. Unless where you came from runs worse than a Perúvian-Bolivian bus line.

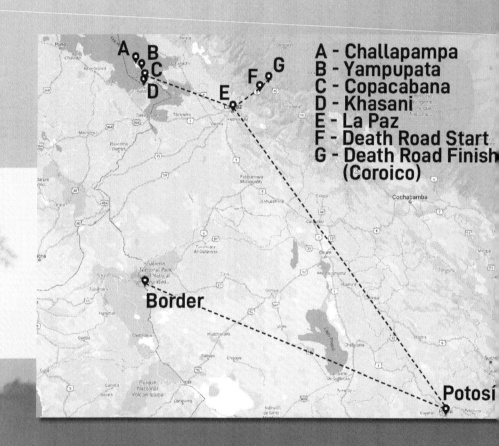

A - Challapampa
B - Yampupata
C - Copacabana
D - Khasani
E - La Paz
F - Death Road Start
G - Death Road Finish
(Coroico)

BOLIVIA

Copacabana
La Paz
Yungas Road
San Pedro Prison
Potosí

REPUBLIC OF BOLIVIA

"In Honor of Simón Bolívar"

At the Perúvian-Bolivian border, it would have been fifty-fifty whether we could have smuggled Ross across. It was a sort of a desolate crossing, not a lot of chaos that would have offered distractions.

Ross was a 6'1", white, blond guy. Immigration might have noticed that he didn't get processed as he mingled amongst the Perúvian men, whose average height was 5'2.63". The twelfth short-est population in the world, just .03" taller than the Vietnamese.

The island of Timor-Leste wins the shortest population coming in at 5'1.28".

Perú immigration was an easy stamp out. Exiting the building, you walked the distance of two football fields across the border to get your stamp into Bolivia. Back on the bus, nobody asked to check that you got your stamps. Not here anyway. At least not today.

COPACABANA

Copacabana was less than impressive. I expected more, but I didn't really know why. Nothing in the guidebook said anything exciting about the town. No backpacker ever mentioned to me how I really must go see Copacabana, Bolivia. No, the town sort of sat there on the shore of Lake Titicaca, wanting to be something. With a chip on its shoulder, it decided it didn't need to impress anyone. Lake Titicaca did that. "Why steal its thunder?" said the town to the gringo.

Rachel was meeting someone, a friend. After asking to join her, I decided that I would do my own thing and meet her in a couple of days. I wanted to be alone and found a room for $1.75. I got them down to $1.45.

It offered a cold concrete floor and dirty gray stucco walls with a single bed and a 50-watt light bulb hung from a wire with a string. Shared toilet and shower. In this town, you could just piss in the alley and no one would give you two looks. Shitting in the street was not uncommon, as I witnessed men doing it throughout South America.

A restaurant near the beach offered only one meal: trout and rice for $1.25. For an additional $0.25, I added a bottle of Paceña beer. I suppose I could have haggled the price a bit. It seemed like

I was the only customer around that day, but I was already up $0.30 on the room.

Trout? In the 1930s, at the request of the Perúvian and Bolivian governments, trout was brought in from the United States for economic purposes. The whole thing backfired, and now trout was one of the most invasive species in southern Perú.

I sat outside on a fold-out chair at a card table with my meal, looking at Lake Titicaca.

I would be remiss to not share with you some of the overly stated statistics about Lake Titicaca, so I'll punch list this:

- The largest lake in South America
- The highest navigable lake in the world
- The birthplace of the Inca and where their spirits return to after death

Yampupata was about a ten-mile hike that would take me about four hours. From there, the plan was to find someone to take me to the Isla del Sol. I assumed finding someone to do this wouldn't be an issue. To be honest, I didn't want to pay the outrageous price of $10 USD to take the established ferry or pay the rumored tax of $2.50 to step foot on the island.

The hike gave me time to reflect about the trip thus far. The things, the people, the places, the adventures, and misadventures. Did Kari ever make it to Santiago? I thought about where my life was just five months ago, in a cubicle working on redlines, reviewing shop drawings, and problem-solving subcontractor hiccups. A landlord, a homeowner. I was stressed, overworked, and putting in seventy-hour weeks. Now I was hiking along the coast of the highest navigable lake in the world in the middle of the world's longest mountain range.

I had seen the Nazca Lines and unusual parades. The wonderful and interesting people I had met from all over the world, and I was just one-third the way down the continent of South America. What if I kept going after South America?

There was Europe, Africa, Australia, Asia—all offering an impossible list of sites and sounds and smells and adventures. New lovers, new friends—perhaps I would meet my wife while hiking the Gobi Desert. Everything was chance, random happenstances.

One minute, I was sitting in a cubicle, and the next, I was haggling over a room in the Andes in a location of the world I never knew existed.

Reader, I can honestly tell you, I didn't see any of this coming.

About an hour into my hike, I met a young kid, maybe thirteen or fourteen. His name was David. He spoke very good English and was hiking to see his grandma, who happened to live in the same direction I was headed. He asked me where I was from and wanted to practice his English. So we walked and talked. He pointed out all the coca and opium fields that surrounded us. We stopped at the Gruta de Lourdes, named after Bernadette Soubirous who had visions of the Immaculate Conception.

The Gruta de Lourdes was a less-than-obvious grotto tucked up into the side of the mountain. Had David not pointed it out, I would have missed the series of metal ladders that led to the statue, covered with simple gifts. At the base of the ladders was an altar where shamans performed their rituals. Another weaving of the Catholic Church with ancestral beliefs.

David told me about how the god Viracocha came out of Lake Titicaca and created the world and the stars and the moon and the sun. Viracocha took a rock and made Manco Capac and Mama Ocllo, the first people in the world and from whom we all come.

Sort of the Adam and Eve story with a different group of actors.

David guided me off the road and onto a trail that involved some climbing. He pointed at the stone path we were walking on. "Inca Trail."

Inca Trail immediately transported one to Machu Picchu, but of course, it would make sense that Inca Trail crisscrossed all over the Andes. In fact, the Qhapaq Ñan, as it was known in Quechua, covered over twenty-five thousand miles of roads, including bridges, tunnels, and causeways.

We reached David's grandma's house and said goodbye.

Down the road a bit, I met a guy who offered to show me his "balsa." Balsas are reed made dating back to the Uru people, who predated the Inca. He told me the Uru still live on islands made from reeds on Lake Titicaca. I had never heard of these floating islands and was fascinated.

Me on the balsa boat.

He then showed me how to use a sling, which was used to hunt or fend off animals to protect the owners' sheep and alpacas.

About a half-mile down the road, I came across a couple from England with the same game plan I had in regards to getting to Isla del Sol.

It didn't take much to find someone to take us. Several men approached us as we got closer to the beach. They all knew they could make a couple of dollars rowing us to the island, which was just shy of a mile away. We chose a boat and pushed off.

"Charon"[34] took us to an undesignated spot on the southeast side of the island and pointed to a path leading up the steep rocky hillside through the terraced farmland.

---

34 The boatman who ferries souls of the dead across the River Styx to Hades.

Following the ridge, we found a small hamlet that offered a couple of hostels. I abandoned the English couple and found a room for three dollars. It was expensive, but I had very few options.

The next day, I hiked the length of the island, along the high ridge amongst the rocks and eucalyptus trees under the gray cloudy sky overlooking the impressive lake.

Reaching the Mesa Ceremónica (Ceremonial Table), which sat in the shadow of the Sacred Rock.

The Mesa Ceremónica was a bit shocking. I thought right away of human sacrifice and black magic. The large, thick flat stone was empty, as if waiting for the next human to be strapped to its cold surface. Arms and legs tied and spread in opposing directions as the group chanted and the shaman dropped the blade. The sun god appeased as the blood of the victim was consumed by the group and the heart, still warm, eaten by the shaman.

I didn't know if any of that actually happened here, but that was where my mind went upon seeing the ceremonial table.

The next day, I wandered down the Inca stairs to the port. I wasn't sure how I was going to get back across the lake. It turned out that if you were on the island, it was assumed you already paid the return fare, so no ticket was required to return on the established ferry I protested taking originally.

Back in Copacabana, I ran into Rachel, who told me Ross had his new passport and was already in La Paz waiting for us. We bought bus tickets and headed out.

An hour out of Copacabana, we arrived at the Strait of Tiquina.

No longer surprised by anything, when we approached the strait and noticed the road just ended into the water, my reaction was simply, huh. I was sure they got this figured out.

Ruta Nacional 2 picked up on the other side of this half-mile waterway. We got off the bus and loaded onto a small passenger boat, which took us across. Along the beach were twenty to thirty floating docks. One pulled up to the water's edge, and we watched as the bus drove onto this makeshift barge. There were at least a half dozen barges heading along both sides of the strait loaded with buses and cows and cars and trucks.

Back on the bus, we reached La Paz just before sunset. The road to La Paz was brown and narrow, lined with random unfinished and uninteresting brown structures.

Beyond the cathedrals and colonial architecture, La Paz was a huge city and all in the shadow of Illimani, a mountain whose height reached 21,122'.

La Paz was all new but all the same. Short, graffiti-covered buildings with metal doors. Quechua women sat on sidewalks while businessmen with poorly constructed suits walked between honking taxis, colectivos, and stray dogs. Garbage lined the streets, moving only when the wind instructed it.

Ross had found us a hostel in the Belén District. Not sure what our next steps were, I found myself sort of complacent. Perhaps it was the gray sky and cool temperature that sort of reminded me of an endless dark fall week in the Midwest. Preparation for winter hibernation. I didn't need to see or do anything, just move on to the next place or not move on. Stay still. Stay quiet. Stay hidden and unknown. I was tired, tired of moving and change. Tired of never completely unloading my backpack to see what it was I was even carrying. Just three days in one place would break this funk. Three days to unpack and repack. Three days to not look for a place to stay, a bus to ride, a meal to eat. Three days.

Instead, I threw my pack on a dorm bed and went for a stroll, finding the Witches' Market, a sort of must-see place according to Lonely Planet. The name was more interesting than the market itself, which was basically a couple of storefronts hosted by a couple of elderly women who sat in chairs waiting to be bothered. Offerings of figurines, aphrodisiac potions, dried herbs, and dried animals (such as snakes and turtles), covered tables, filled baskets, and hung from hooks mounted to the ceiling. Then there were, of course, the famous llama fetuses. It was all stuff that could be found at Marie Laveau's House of Voodoo in New Orleans sans Laveau's touristy offerings of coffee cups, key rings, and t-shirts.

Wealthy Bolivians sacrificed living llamas to the goddess Pachamama[35] to protect their home. Poor Bolivians buried dried llama fetuses under their foundations.

This "witchcraft" reminded me of a book I read in college, *Witchcraft, Oracles, and Magic among the Azande* by E. E. Evans-Pritchard.

The conclusion: Primitive people had a prelogical thought process. If you stubbed your toe or became sick, it wasn't because you were a klutz or just happened to catch a bug. It was because you had been cursed by someone and only a witchdoctor could reverse the "curse."

35 Mother Earth

I bought myself an Inca Cross.

The next day, Rachel asked if I would go with her to the National Bolivian Police Academy. Not entirely clear to me how she pulled this off, but she told me we could get in and ride a couple of horses.

I had just met Sarka the night before. She was from the Czech Republic, and I was now smitten with her. A tough decision had to be made:

- Hang out with Sarka all day and appease the woman I was currently smitten with.
- Ride horses of the Cuerpo de Policía Nacional at the National Bolivian Police Academy.

The horse-riding event was really controlled. We just trotted around a corral for fifteen minutes.

That was it. I'd love to tell you there was more to it. Perhaps I could share with you that we shot machine guns off the backs of the horses as we galloped and jumped through minefields.

But really, all we did was trot around a corral for fifteen minutes, albeit we did this at the National Bolivian Police Academy. "So I got that goin' for me, which is nice."[36]

Before leaving, I asked one of the officers if I could buy his hat. His supervisor wrote down an address where I could buy Bolivian police uniforms. I could get a hat there, which was exactly where we went next. I purchased a Bolivian police baseball cap and a badge, along with a formal policía hat with badge. The vendor selling these items to me didn't even blink an eye.

---

36 *Caddyshack* quote given by Bill Murray's character Carl Spackler.

YUNGAS ROAD

Twenty-three miles long and descending almost 8500', the Yungas Road, aka: Road of Death, Death Road, El Camino de la Muerte, had been christened "The Most Dangerous Road in the World."

When I learned one could ride a mountain bike down it, I cleared my calendar.

For twenty-five dollars, I was given a helmet that was too small, a yellow safety vest, and a shitty, rusty mountain bike. The front suspension was seized, and the brakes, I would learn when trying to avoid going head on into a truck, didn't really function.

Aside from that, I joined a group of seven others and led them down the road. Our leader yelled at me a couple of times for going too fast, but c'mon, it was the road of death! "Drive fast, take chances," "Ride it like you stole it," and all that.

It was really quite beautiful. Starting above the clouds, the road meanders through lush foliage where small waterfalls occasionally drizzled water onto the road.

When the exercise of descending really got nerve-racking was when a truck, bus, or car would suddenly appear around a corner, requiring you to swerve toward the edge. Those were the most dangerous episodes of the descent.

Aside from that, you just needed to be capable of keeping a bike on a ten-foot-wide dirt road. I shouldn't have taken this lightly. Eighteen cyclists had died on this road since 1998. A small number considering the three hundred motorists who died each year.

It wasn't long before we entered the clouds and descended through them, ending at a little hostel in Coroico with a pool.

Yes, I would say it was occasionally harrowing, not being a fan of heights compounded that, but the truly frightening part of the day was when the shuttle drove us back up the Yungas Road, knowing full well other buses and trucks and cars were coming the other way. At first, I sat in my seat like a good boy, but after passing the first truck, I laid down on the floor of the colectivo with my eyes closed, wondering what death felt like when you plummeted from the side of a cliff in a small van.

Yungas Road: "The Road of Death"

CÁRCEL DE SAN PEDRO

San Pedro Prison

Q uite possibly the strangest and most bizarre place I had been to on this journey. I approached a doorway, an arched vestibule. There sat a guard, who I presumed collected your passport. I had a copy of mine, not the original, which was sufficient. My guess was this helped prove you were a "guest," not a prisoner when trying to leave.

The guard opened the gate, and just like that, I was in the courtyard of San Pedro Prison.

It was hard to wrap your head around this being a prison when you saw women hanging laundry out to dry and kids playing fútbol. Women and children in a men's prison? Yep, the families lived together, waiting for the sentence to be served.

There were no guards or police in the prison. The entire operation was run by the inmates. They had their own form of government inside the prison. They manufactured cocaine. One guy showed me his gun, and another a *Crocodile-Dundee*-sized knife.

Cells were sold, not assigned. The more money you had, the nicer cell you could afford.

Had I been more on my game, I could have arranged to stay the night for eight US dollars, but those cells had been rented out for the night to other backpackers from Australia.

The place left me conflicted. Part of me wanted to explore all the nooks and crannies, talk to any of the prisoners who spoke English, and get a better understanding of life in the prison.

The other part of me wanted to get the fuck out of there. I was beginning to doubt that a simple copy of my passport would be my key out of this place.

It was my last night with Sarka. She had a terrible cold, so we talked and drank coca tea. She went to bed early, and I went out, found a street vendor, and tried one of the local favorites, cuy[37] on a stick.

I never saw Sarka again.

37 Guinea pig

POTOSÍ

Potosí claims to be the highest city in the world at 13,420'. It's not. That honor is held by the city of La Rinconada, Perú. Potosí falls somewhere in the teens.

The night bus to Potosí was a long slow journey across Bolivia's Altiplano. Headlights turned off in an effort to save gas, I suppose.

The person next to me was a big fella. We spent the entire night passive aggressively trying to take ownership of the middle armrest while both pretending to be asleep. It ended in a tie.

In Potosí, it was early morning, perhaps seven a.m. I missed my watch and made a note to pick up a new one down the road. Finding a food market, Ross, Rachel, and I had breakfast with the locals and came up with a simple game plan:

- Find room(s)
- Head to the mines at Cerro Rico (Rich Mountain)

There were times I had to get over my anti-tour elitism. To visit the mines at Cerro Rico, I had to suck it up and pay the ten dollars.

It was recommended that we also bring gifts of coca leaves, cigarettes, and dynamite to the miners, which could be found in the shops along the way to the mine.

Turned out, you could buy dynamite for a dollar a stick. I had no clue if that was a deal or not, but it was shocking to think one could just enter a shop and buy sticks of dynamite. Then again, I just bought a Bolivian police cap with a badge.

As we approached, our guide told us that about ten thousand men, women, and children work in the mines. Eight million had died in the mines since they opened because of the lack of oxygen in the tunnels, the dust from explosions, and smoking unfiltered cigarettes. Average life expectancy of a mine worker was forty years old.

Eduardo Galeano wrote in his book, *Open Veins of Latin America*: "You could build a silver bridge from Potosí to Madrid (Spain) from what was mined here—and one back with the bones of those that died taking it out."

We were given hard hats with lamps, rubber boots, yellow rain suit overalls, and heavy windbreakers, then marched into the darkness.

Me, Rachel, and Ross in the Mines at Cerro Rico.

If you are claustrophobic, have a fear of the dark, or just have a strong urge to live, skip this tour. Three of the Australians with us hightailed it out of there in less than five minutes.

The opening was tall, but the passage quickly narrowed and the walls closed in. There was no rhyme or reason to the layout of the honeycomb of passageways. They went up and down rickety wood ladders. They went left and right and sideways. What would a cross section of this look like? Perhaps an ant farm.

Pipes bringing in compressed air hissed around us. Our guide brought us to a statue of the Devil.

The miners believed God should be worshiped when above the ground, but the Devil was the lord of the underworld, the mines below. So they brought him gifts daily to show respect.

The Devil

On August first, llamas were slaughtered in a ritual sacrifice and their blood smeared on the equipment and entrance of the mine. The heart was then placed at the feet of the Devil, and he was given a day to enjoy his feast.

Interesting stuff.

I sat in a cramped tunnel watching a guy hit a chisel with a hammer for ten minutes. He did this all day, every day. At one point, we turned off our head lamps and sat in the darkest darkness, remote sounds of metal hitting metal hitting rock echoed around the labyrinth of tunnels.

On the way out, I helped a young kid, maybe twelve, push a wheelbarrow of rocks out of the mine. I took my helmet off and watched as he dumped the rocks and went back into the darkness for more rocks. When I was twelve, I was learning algebra. He was entering and exiting a small opening in a mountain in the Bolivian high plains.

One day, he'd graduate from removing rocks with a wheelbarrow to chiseling them until he died in roughly twenty-eight years, statistically speaking.

Keeping a couple of sticks of dynamite for ourselves, Ross and I decided to light the fuses and throw them into the empty landscape. Quite an explosive experience.

This would be our last day together. Ross and Rachel would head back to La Paz to meet their parents, then return to the United States.

I heard Ross went and joined the United States Army, and Rachel, who had been on a three-month leave of absence, went back to her job as a smokejumper.

On the bus to Arica, I cracked open a newly acquired book from the hostel, *The Alchemist* by Paulo Coelho.

It was a fast, short read with a captivating and simple story that pulled me in. The only time I stopped to enjoy the outside world was when we passed the dormant volcano Nevado del Sajama. The highest point in Bolivia at 21,463', the white-capped volcano stood guard.

REPÚBLICA DE CHILE

Arica
Santiago
Puerto Montt
Navimag
Puerto Natales
Torres del Paine
Bus to Ushuaia

REPÚBLICA DE CHILE

"Where the Land Ends"

B y the time we hit the border at Chile, I was halfway through my book. As we exited the bus for immigration, I looked forward to getting back to see how the story played out.

The border control entering Chile was a remote, unassuming, lonely building that rested in the shadow of the snowcapped Andes at 15,300'.

The landscape was endless, cold, and empty. Life seemed impossible, yet Polylepis and Copiapoa managed to emerge from the hard rocks, dotting the landscape to prove their toughness against this rugged Altiplano.

North of the border control stood K'isi K'isini at an impressive 18,100'. Just north of that was Volcán Parinacota and Pomerape, each standing just shy of 21,000', dominating the visible range.

South was the volcano Uqi Uqini, all alone at 18,100'.

The ununiformed police officer waved at me to approach. His female assistant instructed me to put my packs on the table and open them.

"Shit!" I saw my bag of coca leaves being revealed as she pulled items out of my bag.

Was it illegal to have coca leaves in Chile? Would they arrest me or simply throw it away? I overthought the potential outcome of my situation while playing it cool. If they asked me, I'd be like, "I don't know, just some leaves." I didn't think the old line of "I was holding it for a friend" would work. It never worked on my dad when he would find my stash of beer(s).

She pulled out the Perúvian police officer hat and showed it to her superior. He was currently looking at the Bolivian police officer cap I was carrying. They both laughed and asked how I came to have them. The Perúvian cap still had the note from the police officer, so I showed him that and told them about the store in La Paz where anyone could buy policía uniforms apparently.

They took a photo of themselves with the hats and instructed me to repack my stuff.

He handed back the hats with a smile, shaking his head in disbelief that I had them.

"Do you have a hat I can buy?" I asked him before leaving the control zone.

"Haha. NO!"

Back on the bus, we descended an impressive seventeen thousand feet through the Atacama. The driest desert in the world was often used by NASA as a testing ground for equipment to be used in space.

About thirty miles east of Arica, we dropped into the Valle de Lluta, where the Lluta River allowed for the farming of onions and potatoes before dumping into the Pacific Ocean.

ARICA

Arriving in "the very illustrious and royal city of San Marcos of Arica," as it was once called, was a thawing process. It was the driest inhabited city on the planet, receiving an average of .03" of rain a year. I felt like I had been cold for months, and the fact was, I had been. The high Andes and Altiplano were dry, cold, windy, harsh landscapes. Arica, too, was dry, but it was warm, oh so warm, reaching the low eighties with plenty of sunshine.

After finding a room to stay, I bought some Escudo beer and plopped myself down at Playa El Gringo, a well-known spot for surfing. There I soaked up the sun and suds and watched the people play in the surf. This was not a time for cultural experiences. It was a decompression time.

It was the first time I had been alone since México D.F., and I had no desire to insert a new temporary friend into the mix. I didn't have the energy to hear their story or repeat mine. I thought about *The Alchemist*. The boy's story was very relatable. It was the hero's journey.

Reader, if you have not read this book and want to read it without spoiling the book for yourself, **STOP HERE**, skip the next page and start back in at: **START HERE**.

The boy leaves home. The boy encounters dangers, overcomes challenges, and eventually returns home only to find the treasure he was looking for was there all along.

It was the hero's journey which your hero was on. I was at the transformation phase. Reaching California on my bike was my death and rebirth. Death to who I was and rebirth to who I was transforming into. No, not transforming into—I was polishing my shine.

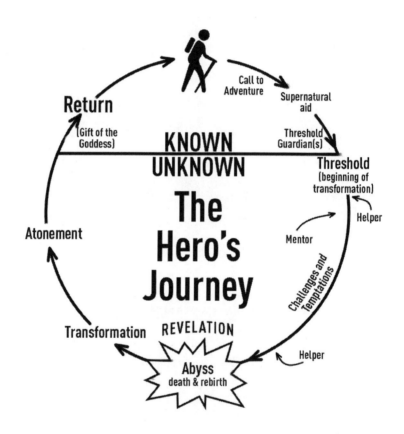

START HERE:

Your hero was still on his hero's journey. Taking the long way home, I had overcome the great challenges and hardships of riding across the United States. The abyss/revelation/death/rebirth was behind me. A break-up, quitting my job, and riding across the Great Plains, Rocky Mountains, alkaline desert,[38] and Sierra Nevadas to prove to myself I could do something I never thought I could.

After three days of thawing, drinking, and meandering the quiet coastal city, I decided to fly to Santiago rather than spend a day and a half riding on a bus, fighting for the center armrest, and listening to *Rambo III* dubbed in Spanish played at volume eleven.

Flying from Arica to Santiago was a time saver. To put the distance in perspective, it would be like flying from:

USA:	Minneapolis to New York City
Europe:	London to Rome
Australia:	Brisbane to Adelaide
India:	Mumbai to New Delhi
Africa/Middle East:	Cairo to Dubai
Russia:	Moscow to Omsk

38 Mojave Desert

SANTIAGO

"Named after St. James of the Bible"

There was no doubt that Santiago and the surrounding area had a lot to offer.

My departure date to Antarctica was approaching, and I didn't want to miss the boat.

I did have two items on my agenda. One was to have one thousand dollars wired to me via Western Union as my debit card was now useless.

After collecting my money, I would visit the Concha y Toro vineyard, which now had a whole new meaning.

The exchange rate at the time was about seven hundred Chilean pesos to the dollar. The one thousand US dollars I went to pick up at the Western Union was given to me in converted pesos. I was now in possession of seven hundred thousand Chilean pesos.

Three hundred thousand shy of being a millionaire.

I found a room at a house. I was not quite in the mood to engage a bunch of backpackers, although I'm sure it would have been fun.

Taking a taxi to the vineyard, I was able to join the last group of the day. A group of sixty plus US Americans.

The tour was fine. I enjoyed the story behind the name of one of their collections of wine called, Casillero del Diablo (Cellar of the Devil).

The story?

> The owner of the winery hid his prized collection of wines for his own use down in his secret cellar.
>
> Over time, he noticed his wine was disappearing from his secret cellar. Fully aware the people were superstitious, he started a rumor that at night, strange events were happening around his place. Those strange events were the work of the devil who lived in his cellar.
>
> His wine was no longer tampered with, and a new line of wine was created.

Now what I'm about to tell you isn't my way of belittling tourists. I was a tourist. I am a tourist. But you know there is always that ONE person. That one person, in this case, was a woman from Iowa.

Guide: "These grapes to the left, these are very very special grapes, and they are all picked carefully by hand."

Group murmuring: "Oh wow, by hand, hmm that's a lot of grapes, isn't that something?"

Guide: "These grapes in the middle, these are very good grapes and are picked by hand and machine."

Group murmuring: "Oh, wow, look at all those grapes, Bob, can you see that, let me take a picture."

Guide: "These grapes to the right, these we pick by machine and use for our mass-produced wines. Any questions?"

Iowa woman: "Yes, with the grapes to the left, what kind of machine do they use to pick those?"

Guide: "Only by hand."

Iowa woman: "But what kind of machine?"

Guide: "They are very delicate grapes. We only picked by hand."

She thought for a while. "I bought a bottle of Concha y Toro for thirty-five dollars. Now, is that the most I can spend?"

Annoyed, I chimed in with absolutely nothing to lose, "Lady, I'll sell you a bottle for $135 if you want."

With that, we were in the gift shop, tasting wines. The wine tasting was free. I entered with the back half of the group, anticipating the possibility of running into Kari, who would scold me for making her wait for so long.

After ten, maybe fifteen minutes, the bus driver entered the room and told everyone to get on the bus. That left me and the three employees in the gift shop with a bunch of open wine bottles. It was closing time.

"Don't you need to get on the bus?" they asked.

"Nope, I came here by taxi. I'm on my own." Looking around at all the opened, half-consumed bottles of wine used for sampling, I had to ask, "So, what are you going to do with all these open bottles of wine?"

"We're going to drink them. Here, take a glass and join us."

International relations between Chile and the United States improved dramatically that afternoon.

✫

Walking around the Plaza de Armas with a solid buzz, I approached a group of four young twenty-something-year-olds covered in tattoos and facial piercings, listening to Chilean Punk music.

At some point along the way, I decided I wanted to get a tattoo. I had been working on some sketch that I thought captured who I had become since leaving Minneapolis on the bicycle.[39] It was a sort of surrealistic set of curved lines that was meant to symbolize my free spirit.

"¿Habla English?" I asked.

"No," said the group's fearless leader, giving me a "piss off, move on, pendejo" look.

"¿Dónde es…" I pointed to one of the guys' arms covered in tattoos. "Yo quiero… um… tattoo?"

In Spanish, it's pronounced "Tat-eww-wa-ta." Just like that, they suddenly spoke English and wrote down the address for the tatuaje parlor on a piece of paper.

With my sketch, I entered the tattoo parlor. Two other guys were getting back tattoos, one of Mayan glyphs.

I decided I wanted to get mine on my right back shoulder. Originally, I wanted it centered on my back, but then realized I wouldn't be able to reach it to apply the healing cream given to me after the trauma.

After pulling off my shirt, I handed the tattoo artist my sketch. He took it, marked it on my shoulder, dipped the needle in the ink,

39 TBATB

and then the buzzing started. Your hero immediately broke into a cold sweat. I didn't like needles, and this was precisely why I didn't have a tattoo. He finished the outline of the smallest curved line.

"Fin," I said.

"No, amigo."

"¡No! ¡Fin!" I wasn't asking, I was trying to say, "I'm done, it hurts. Thanks for all the fun, keep the five bucks."

"No no." He brought a mirror over so I could see he was, in fact, not done.

"Sí, amigo. Entiendo. Pero yo fin. No más," I said in a jumbled mess of Spanish.

The tattoo artists. Their fingers are modeling their work.

And that was how your hero ended up with a weird wavy-lined, five-dollar tattoo on his shoulder.

TO PUERTO MONTT

Everything seemed to come to life as the bus traveled south. After leaving the harsh, dry Atacama Desert, I was now on a bus traveling through the most wonderful, lush landscape.

It reminded me of the United States Midwest. No, it was more like Europe with its metric speed limit signs, overpass signs, and lack of billboards.

Ruta 5, also known as the Pan-American Sur, was four lanes wide with a median, possibly the safest stretch of road I'd been on since touching foot on this continent. Evergreens and beech trees gave cover as the cows and sheep grazed behind barbed-wire fences all under a heavy grayish sky.

Buildings switched from partially constructed brick and stucco mud-colored boxes to wood-sided buildings with tin roofs. Void of any unwanted artwork, there was a noticeable lack of garbage. Even the vehicles seemed cleaner.

Approaching Puerto Montt to the east was Osorno volcano, capped with snow. The tree line was lower here, around 3100'. Bolivia boasted the highest tree line in the world at 17,100'.

To compare:
- Rocky Mountain National Park: 12,000'
- Swiss Alps: 7200'
- Urals: 3600'

Puerto Montt sat on the northern end of Reloncaví Sound in the northern part of the Chilean fjords.

The air was cooler and crisper, and the smell of the sea was front and center.

I was in Patagonia now. A distant land that I would never have imagined I'd ever have the pleasure to step foot on.

NAVIMAG

Somewhere along the way I had heard about taking a ferry through the fjords of Chile. The ferry, I was told, departed from Puerto Montt and took you to Puerto Natales.

From there, you could hike Torres del Paine, which at the time I was buying my ferry ticket, I knew nothing about. I just wanted to try something different and a ferry through the fjords ticked off that box.

The other option was a thirty-hour bus ride down the famous Ruta 40.

Boarding for the ferry started at nine a.m.

The Navimag Ferry took cars, bikes, animals, food, supplies, and trucks, and had a few beds for passengers.

The ferry was weather-beaten. Rust grew from the many layers of paint applied over the years. I bought the cheapest ticket and in exchange got a windowless bunk in the belly of the ferry, a curtain for privacy, and three simple meals a day.

Everything I needed.

Navimag Ferry

There were a total of seven of us heading to Puerto Natales. One Swiss woman who, like me, was traveling on her own. The other five seemed to know each other but possibly had met along the way. All but one was from Australia. The one not from Australia was from Bristol, UK.

Once aboard and settled in, everyone collected on the deck as we set sail.

It wasn't long before the Swiss woman and I inserted ourselves into the group, and then, we were seven.

It also wasn't long before I was in love. She was a short redhead from Perth, Australia. Feisty, funny, and rolled her own cigarettes. She'd been traveling around South America alone until she met the other four at a hostel in Santiago.

I envisioned what my life with her was going to be like. We'd leave South America and return to her homeland. We'd buy a ranch in the Australian Outback and raise sheep and a family, perhaps two kids, maybe three if she was up for it. It would be a fine, simple life.

We drifted past the mysterious island of Chiloé. Being an Art Bell fan, I recalled hearing about Chiloé and its legend of male warlocks, or brujos.

These brujos liked to do things like live in caves, kidnap and mutilate children, and terrorize the locals.

To become a brujo, one had to:

- De-baptize oneself in a waterfall for forty days.
- Make a pact with the Devil (par for the course I suppose).
- Kill someone close to you and use their skin to cover your spell book.

Once that was done, you would have shape-shifting abilities and the power to cast spells and curses.

To the east was Corcovado National Park, the crisp white-capped mountains descended into a lush green forest until reaching the ripple-less coastline.

That night, we played cards and drank Gato Negro wine.

The captain kept us in the channel for most of the day, which meant the waters were calm and serene. Those calm waters got choppy when we turned out to sea for a short while.

It might be true to say some of us had a bit of seasickness. The ocean teeter-tottered the ship for what seemed like days, but really was only an hour, perhaps two. The waves weren't huge by any means, but they did let us know they were there.

Back in the channel, we came across a family sailing on a forty-five-foot sailboat. They waved us down. The dad and his four-teen-year-old daughter pulled up to the ferry in their Zodiac and boarded. The Swiss woman in our new group of seven knew the family and decided to go with them to Ushuaia, leaving the six of us to fend for ourselves.

The family had been sailing around the world for three years. The kids were gaining life experiences and an education I couldn't possibly comprehend.

Curious events such as these didn't even phase me anymore. In Santiago, I met two guys from California who were kayaking the Futaleufú River.

After telling them about how I biked to Truckee, California, they asked whose wedding I went to. Turned out, they not only knew the groom of the wedding, but they also knew my cousin Amy's boyfriend who I had just built a fence with.[40]

That night, we played hide-and-seek and drank Gato Negro wine.

The fjords continued to impress us as we floated south passing the rusty, guano-covered[41] wreck of *MV Capitán Leonidas*, a freighter that ran aground on the Bajo Cotopaxi in 1963.

That night, we planned our hike of Torres del Paine and drank Gato Negro wine.

40 TBATB
41 Accumulated excrement of seabirds

PUERTO NATALES

We found probably one of the most run-down ramshackle hostels I'd ever stayed at, and I'd stayed at some run-down ramshackle places.

Tilting hard to stage right, I'd give it another two months before the hostel simply collapsed. Windows were boarded up. Inside was cold and dark, mattresses were on the floor. No effort was made to make the place appealing.

Had it not been decided by the group of five (before I joined), I would have preferred to camp along the water's edge, but the hostel was cheap and protected us from the hard winds Patagonia was known for.

We gathered supplies at the grocery store, agreeing to just get stuff for ourselves so as not to debate what sort of sauce everyone wanted on their pasta. We did agree to share coffee. I just grabbed a few fresh baguettes, some cheese, and a few dry-cured Spanish chorizo.

That night, we drank Gato Negro wine.

When I first saw Torres del Paine, it was a stunningly impressive sight. The massive two-toned granite rock demanded respect. As if it exploded through the soft Magellanic subpolar forest, cutting its way upward with its jagged edges. Nothing about it seemed to fit in with the rest of the surroundings. The deep valleys held mysteries that begged to be solved but were better left alone.

Torres del Paine meant Tower of Blue. Paine was from the native Tehuelche language, which was spoken by the Aónikenk people. The language died in 2019 along with Dora Manchado, the last of the Aónikenks.

We hiked up to our first campsite, Torres Campsite, set up our tents, and then completed the day with a physically exerting hike up to Mirador Las Torres.

I suppose we ate our dessert first and should have saved visiting Mirador Las Torres last, as a sort of reward for the fifty miles we were about to hike. It was all so epic, the three granite towers holding court over a lake surrounded by a boulder field. I clamored over some rocks, looking at the three giants from various angles.

Back at camp, I ate my simple meal. It was then we realized a major oversight. No one brought any Gato Negro wine.

The next day, the hike was a nice and easy nine to ten miles. We decided on Camping Italiano, which was virtually empty, and did a pack-less day hike up Britanico Viewpoint.

Group photo, Torres del Paine

As we trekked, we'd come across the occasional hiker. Typically, our group stepped out of the way for others, depending on who was leading. Every time we passed people, one of the guys in our group would say, "De nada." They would look confused most of the time and reply with "Buenos días."

After a few hours of hiking, I had to ask, "Steve, why do you say, 'de nada'?"

"Because it's nice to say."

"What do you think *de nada* means?"

He looked at me like I should already know this.

"Cory, it means *good day.*"

Everyone in the group busted out laughing.

"Dude, it means *you're welcome.* Actually, it's more like, *no problem, it's nothing.*"

He looked confused and turned to the group he boarded the ferry with. "Why didn't you guys tell me this?! I've been saying *de nada* since Santiago."

"We thought it was funny."

From Italiano to Refugio and Camping Grey was an eleven-mile haul that started off pretty innocently and then turned more challenging as the trail ascended into the forest along the east coast of Lago Grey. Since we arrived in the park, the weather was absolutely perfect and would continue to be throughout the entire trek.

Arriving at campsite Grey, we met two other hikers from Montana. Aside from that, the hike along the coast of Lago Grey was almost void of any other trekkers.

From campsite Grey, you had a clear view of Glacier Grey. It stood almost one hundred feet tall and over three miles wide. A couple of small icebergs calved by the glacier dotted the lake. They drifted by us with no sense of urgency. After millions of years stuck in a glacier, they were finally free. I set my tent up along the coast.

Campsite across from Glacier Grey

While preparing dinner, a park ranger arrived and told us there was a fire near the trail, or on the trail. It wasn't entirely clear. He ordered us not to hike tomorrow but to wait and a boat would come by to pick us up in the morning. He would camp with us and serve as a conduit for any new information.

"You tired of the bread, cheese, and meat, Cory?"

"No, not really. Look forward to a nice dinner when we get somewhere."

"You want some tuna? I have an extra tin."

When I was a kid, we had this lady, Mrs. Hook, who would occasionally watch us during the day. I didn't like her at all. She wouldn't let us play outside and closed all the blinds and shutters in the house to keep the sunlight out. She would dice up hot dogs and mix them with macaroni and cheese, which, as a ten-year-old, I was fully aware of the sort of culinary sin that was. But the worst was when she made tuna fish sandwiches. I couldn't stand the smell of tuna fish sandwiches and refused to eat them. Up until now, this very moment camped out at Lago Grey, I had never tasted tuna simply due to the association.

But the offer was given, and I had just eaten a guinea pig not too long ago, so I pulled open the top and grabbed a spork.

The tuna was sealed in olive oil, and it was magical. I was hooked, devouring the tin, soaking up the oil and scraps with my baguette. From that day forward, tinned tuna in olive oil became a staple.

The next day, the news went from good to bad to good to bad. One minute we could hike out, then a new message on the walkie talkie would tell us to stay and a boat was coming. This went on and on for about four hours. Finally, we got the green light. Along the way back to Lake Pehoé, we came across a group of park rangers with shovels and axes putting out a small smoldering patch of the Magellanic subpolar forest.

It was a fragile ecosystem, and these things were taken very seriously.

Three years later, in 2005, a Czech tourist sparked a fire with a stove in an unauthorized area that destroyed 7 percent of the park.

From Lake Pehoé, we took a ferry to where the buses waited for any hikers leaving the park. We jumped on the last bus, and in two hours, we were back at our shack of a hostel.

There was no airport in Puerto Natales, so aside from the ferry, the only way out was to hitch or bus. Cindy, the Australian redhead, and I headed south to Punta Arenas. She was flying out in two days to attend Carnaval in Salvador, Brazil. After that, she was headed to London for a year to work. I'd see her off and keep heading south to Ushuaia.

I was a bit heartbroken when she left, no lie. Was it because I was in love with her? Or perhaps I was in love with the idea of being in love? I sorted through what I wanted in a relationship and what I needed to give to make that relationship work.

A relationship on the road wouldn't last. We were not living a life that was real. Maybe we were, but what if this traveling from one place to another ended up stopping and we decided to go back to the nine-to-five? There would be mortgages, car payments, work stress, perhaps kids to feed. In the case of Cindy, sheep to sheer on our ranch in Perth. Would we handle stress the same or different? Would I be supportive? Would she?

Or maybe not. Maybe we would never return to that nine-to-five. Why would we? Why should we? There were no rules to life.

Relationships started and ended fast when you were backpacking around. The people you met were like-minded, adventurous, independent, and for the most part, likable. They might or might not be trying to work through some personal stuff. We were all easy targets for fleeting romances.

But I did like Cindy. I told her I needed to hammer out a few items back in the United States and be in London this summer. "Our relationship would blossom like a rose garden," I told myself.

Then we'd move to Australia and start that ranch.

Punta Arenas was a depressing place, mostly because of my mood. But moods were as fleeting as romances.

The bus to Ushuaia was about twelve hours. Next to me were two Israeli women.

What I had learned talking with Israelis traveling around South America was once they graduated from high school, they were obligated to join the military for a length of time, men serving a bit longer than women.

Once their service was complete, they took a six-month break. "Hatyul Ha'Gadol," which meant "The Great Trip." A hero's journey to go out, face experiences, overcome challenges, and return a better, stronger person.

The two most popular avenues traveled:

"Gringo Trail" – South and Central America in search of trekking and outdoor adventures.

"Hummus Road" – India and Southeast Asia in search of relaxation and spiritual enlightenment.

These two were freshly discharged from the Israeli army. We struck up a conversation that included two other women from Australia, all in their early twenties.

The conversation ebbed and flowed until one of the Australians asked the Israelis if they planned to visit Australia.

"NO WAY!"

"Really, why? It's wonderful."

"Way too dangerous."

The Australians were a little taken aback by that.

"Too dangerous? You guys live in Israel."

"Yes, but Australia is way too dangerous."

The other Israeli jumped in: "You guys have spiders that can kill you, you have snakes that can kill you, you have fish that can kill you, you have crocodiles that can kill you, and you can't swim in the ocean because sharks will kill you."

"Well, yeah, but you guys… you guys have rockets and bombs exploding all the time. I mean, if you were sitting at a bus stop, any car could be a bomb and explode and kill you."

One Israeli said, "Well, that's just day-to-day living, nothing to be concerned about."

"Like every country that surrounds you wants to kill you. Why don't you guys take some desert from us out in the Outback and call it Israel? We're pretty nice people in Australia."

From Punta Arenas, you went northeast, which seemed counterintuitive since Ushuaia was southeast. To get onto the island of Tierra del Fuego, you had to cross the Strait of Magellan and the narrowest part was between Punta Delgada and Punta Espora. The crossing was a bit more advanced than the one in Bolivia, as a proper car ferry was used.

Land of Fire, Tierra del Fuego, was divided almost down the middle between Chile and Argentina.

During Pinochet's regime, over 290 minefields along the borders of Perú, Bolivia, and Argentina were created. Roughly a million land mines were placed in total.

I read that most were cleared, but on more than one occasion, I saw signs that read:

PELIGRO CAMPO MINADO

DANGER MINE FIELD

GEFAHR MINENFELD

Paso San
Sabastian

Ushuaia

REPÚBLICA ARGENTINA: "LAND OF SILVER"

Ushuaia
Trek with Hans

REPÚBLICA ARGENTINA

"Land of Silver"

A t San Sebastián, we crossed into Argentina. Another large sign with a slightly different message declared: "Las Malvinas son Argentinas," in reference to the islands we knew as the Falkland Islands, which were located three hundred miles east of Argentina and almost eight thousand miles southwest of London, England, as the crow flies. The Falklands, or Islas Malvinas, had been "ruled" by the French, British, Spanish, and Argentinians since their discovery. In 1833, the British asserted its sovereignty over the islands, while at the same time, Argentina claimed ownership of them.

One hundred forty-nine years later, perhaps after a few shots of vodka, the president of Argentina, Leopoldo Fortunato Galtieri Castelli, thought it a good idea to attack the islands and start the Falklands War.

The long and short of it. After seventy-four days of war:
- 649 Argentinians were killed, 1,657 were wounded, 11,313 were captured
- 255 British were killed, 775 were wounded, 115 were captured
- 3 civilians were killed by "friendly" fire
- British claimed victory

Argentina accepted defeat; however, from the looks of the "Las Malvinas son Argentinas" signs, they did not, and have not, accepted it gracefully.

Not being entirely up on the local news of the day, what with being on a ferry through the fjords and hiking Torres del Paine and staying off the internet as it really wasn't a big thing back in 2002, I wasn't aware of Argentina's current financial situation.

USHUAIA

A rriving in Ushuaia and finding a hostel, I learned from the owner, Sabastian, that he had no idea what to charge for a night because the Argentinian peso exchange rate was unknown. One minute it was one to one with the dollar, then it was one US dollar to ten pesos.

The Argentinian financial market was crushed. No money at the banks. If you had a million pesos, they might only be worth one hundred thousand dollars. Even so, the banks limited what you could withdrawal.

Unemployment was at 25 percent. To make money, Argentinians found work picking up garbage and collecting cardboard to sell to recycling plants. The prize on one of the popular TV game shows was offering the winner a job as a janitor.

Sabastian approached the whole situation with, "Pay me whatever, whenever."

I settled in and sort of became a resident at the hostel, having a bit of time on my hands before heading off to Antarctica. I kept myself busy with morning hikes up the Glacier Martial, which overlooked the town, the Beagle Channel, and the white-capped mountains on Isla Navarino.

I started to help Sabastian out around the hostel. He was from Germany and overstayed his visa by a few years. Showing me his passport one evening, with his very expired visa, he put his finger over his mouth. "Shhhh, Sabastian is illegal."

Out in search of tinned tuna, I ran into a familiar face. It was the daughter of the guy from the sailboat who picked up the Swiss girl while we traveled through the fjords.

"Hey, aren't you traveling with your family? Sailing around the world? I met you in the fjords a week or so ago."

She remembered me. "Yes, I remember. We are here doing some repairs." She had a bag of small engine parts and electrical knickknacks.

"How was the trip down?" I worked on some small talk and was just sort of in awe of her. She didn't bite.

"It's fine. We are busy. Lots of work to do on the boat and homework."

"What do you have there?"

"We had some electrical issues… just some parts for the…" She went into an electrical engineering language I didn't speak.

"Wow, you know how to do all that?"

"My dad shows me and my brother. I can fix pretty much most mechanical and electrical problems on the boat. Look, I got to go." She studied the clouds. "The temperature dropped, and the atmospheric pressure is changing. I've been watching those clouds build up pretty quickly from the west. They are moving pretty fast, and I noticed all the birds are taking shelter. Need to get back before the storm hits."

I watched her run across the street toward the harbor and thought: *There will never be a man or woman out there who will ever meet the expectations she will require in a partner.*

Looking up at the sky, I thought, *Pffft, of course I noticed the birds taking shelter.*

TREK WITH HANS

I t was a Sunday evening when I first met Hans. He was a tall, thin, quiet guy from Holland who was easy to talk with. He had a bag of hash that he smuggled in with him from Holland and was looking for someone to enjoy it with him. Looking for someone to share your weed or hash or shrooms with in a hostel anywhere in the world isn't a difficult task. We hit it off pretty quickly.

His plan was to do some trekking, and after about an hour of conversation, he asked if I'd join him. We agreed to leave in the morning, 9:00 a.m. sharp. He had a hike in mind. At the time, I don't think the trek had a name. If it did, we didn't know about it. I didn't even know how Hans knew about. The trek was known as the Sierra Valdivieso Circuit. Twenty-eight miles long with 6300' of elevation gain.

Rolling a joint, Hans said it would take three days. Let me repeat that: Hans said it would take three days.

Day 1 of 3

I found Hans, hungover, sitting with his backpack at the ready. He was smoking and having a breakfast of toast and coffee.

"Oh shit, am I going trekking with you today?"

"Yes." He smiled. "I'll wait." He knew I wasn't packed.

Okay. Three-day trek, what did I need: tent, sleeping bag, extra pair of socks, hat, jacket, and gloves. I wouldn't need a change of clothes.

Groceries: I bought eight tins of tuna, a couple baguettes, two blocks of cheese, some dried salami, and three liters of water.

It was around 9:30 a.m. when we finally walked out the door and started our four-mile hike to the trailhead.

I knew it was nine-thirty because I bought a new watch for an outrageous amount of money at the only outdoor equipment store in Ushuaia. Taxes on electronics in South America meant you paid twice the amount for the product than you would pay in the United States.

The Casio Pro Trek Triple Sensor was a monster of a watch that not only told the time but also did all the usual things, like stopwatch, timer, etc. It also had a compass, altimeter, barometer, thermometer, and was water resistant up to 200 meters (656 feet) according to the marketing literature. Far deeper than my deepest dive of 120 feet, but could it survive a free dive with Herbert Nitsch?[42]

We hiked along the road to the trail for about four miles and then managed to get a ride for the last four miles. It was an overcast gray day. I didn't notice any birds taking shelter, so concerns of rain were abolished.

The trail started off easy enough, along a well-traveled hard-packed stretch of dirt. Then we came upon a pile of bones. The trail ended at the edge of a large, peat moss bog. A sure sign to turn around

42 Known as "the deepest man on earth," world record holder for freediving 253 meters (831 feet).

Contemplating the hike we were about to take.

We both agreed, looking at the map Hans had, that the mountains beyond the bog were where we wanted to go and pressed forward through a mile of shin-deep peat moss. Every step was a struggle and an exercise in trying to keep your shoes from being sucked off, lost forever in this massive bog in the land of fire. The ground under the peat was uneven. We tripped and fell frequently, and by the end of it, we were drenched from shoulders to toes.

We aimed for one of several valleys in front of us, the middle and widest valley making the most sense to shoot for. The topographical map was completely useless. The contour lines were too distant and offered no understandable detail of the terrain. One could hardly tell the difference between the flat areas and the mountains. This would be a trailblazing exercise.

Occasionally, we found a footprint in the mud and that was enough to keep us moving forward.

Our first day ended with a climb up some steep rocks and what felt like a half-mile struggle through dense vegetation that clawed at our every move, hampering any sort of speedy progress.

Eventually we found a small clearing that was relatively flat and set up camp. After our tents were set up and food prepared, I was happily surprised to see Hans produce a box of wine.

We didn't talk much that evening. Both a little wiped out, we sat in our wet clothes, ate our dinners, and drank wine until the sunset.

Day 2 of 3

Hans rolled his own cigarettes and liked to take his time in the morning, enjoy a smoke and some coffee, slowly and carefully pack everything up. I preferred to get up, pack up, and get going. This was the biggest compatibility issue we had.

We did a little recon without our packs and realized we were a bit off from where we should be, or at least, where we thought we should be as there was not a designated trail.

Correcting our direction, the day started with a hike up a long ascent. Not steep or particularly difficult, just long. In three hours, we reached the tree line, which in this part of the world was 1950'.

Skirting a small nameless lake, we continued to ascend a scree field to the top of our first pass.

Having no clue how far we had hiked, we did know, from some notes Hans had about the hike, that the first pass was seven miles from the trailhead. Rather pathetic how long seven miles had taken us.

I looked at Hans. "Three days?" He rolled his cigarette and gave me a smile.

Descending the pass, we pressed through thick forest with steep declines. Often slipping, I would hear Hans shout "God almighty" as we struggled through the dense flora.

The forest eventually thinned out and we found ourselves oftentimes trekking through knee deep swamps created by beaver dams.

Beavers were a major problem here in Tierra del Fuego. The Argentinian government decided that they wanted to start a fur trade industry. In 1946, fifty beavers were released into the wild. Now it was estimated there were over two hundred thousand, and they were destroying the landscape and protected trees. The dams were destroying grazing pastures. For Hans, it was the science behind these dams that kept him fascinated.

Every beaver dam we came across, Hans would stop and study it, sharing with me the details of the dam. Calculating things like volume and square meters and pressure and force.

"How do you know all this about dams?"

"I was a professor of hydrology in Rotterdam before coming here."

Sometimes, when explaining the science behind the structures, he would default to his native tongue and talk to me in Dutch. I responded with the occasional, "uh-huh."

Then, after a few hours I heard it. "Cory! Stop! I can't go any further."
We found a flat area near a waterfall in an open field of tall grass and
set up camp.

Taking a rest.

Day 3 of 3

It poured throughout the night. Sheets of rain and strong winds
zipped through the valley in waves.

I watched my barometer on my new Casio to see if it was
changing, but the number stayed the same, and the rain kept coming. I killed time naming all the states in the United States and
then their capitals.

It was almost noon when the winds and the rain stopped.

Hans emerged from his tent, sat on his backpack, and rolled his cigarette. We took our time preparing a late breakfast while allowing our tents to dry under what was now a clear blue sky.

We continued north and moved up another ascending valley, this time along a creek which was framed with thick foliage. Once again, we found ourselves above the tree line where we stopped for lunch.

Looking at the map, we knew at some point we needed to go up one of these steep scree-laden mountains to the west. It was just really hard to know which one. The key feature we were looking for and should come across was a mountain lake named Lago Azul. Which we both assumed would be a very blue lake based on its name and the notes Hans had which said, "we would know it when we see it."

Studying our options and our surroundings, we finally agreed on which mountain we would ascend.

I led the way. Choosing a landmark, I found a lonely bush and went to it. Once reached, I found a boulder as my next landmark and went for that. With the zigging and zagging ascending this mountain of scree, you needed to home in on a landmark.

Although not 100 percent proven, it is said that those who hike where no trails are and use no landmarks to guide them end up hiking in circles. Some say it's because one leg is longer than the other, some say it's because we have a dominant eye that misaligns us, and others say human tendency is to make a right turn when coming across obstacles, like a tree or stones.

Whatever the real reason, my experience has been to find a landmark and aim for it. The line to the landmark may not be straight, but your direction will be true.

About an hour into our ascent, a snow blizzard came out of nowhere. One minute it was clear and sunny, and the next our visibility dropped to just a few feet. I lost sight of Hans, and we both found ourselves completely exposed on the side of a mountain. We had no choice but to wait it out. Yelling over the winds, we agreed if after thirty minutes the storm didn't let up, we would descend back down and try again later.

As quickly as the blizzard appeared, it suddenly was gone. Looking down to the south, I saw a large plateau. In the center of the plateau was a small, yet very intense blue lake.

I felt no need to ask if this was the proverbial "Singing Bush." This had to be Lago Azul.

The climb down was just as slow and daunting with the loose scree and steep slope. In the end, we survived although injured. Hans had punctured his hand on a sharp stone after a fall, and I had a nasty cut on my knee.

By the time we had set up camp and cooked dinner, all the snow had melted.

That night, out of the blue, Hans told me his story about why he was in South America. Sharing didn't appear to come naturally for him.

"A while ago, I was at a concert in Amsterdam. I met a girl, and that night, well, nine months later, she had a baby girl. I told her I wanted to be part of our daughter's life, but she didn't seem to think that was a good idea. I spent the last six months fighting for visitation rights in the courts and finally won. In Holland anyway. After the decision was made, she took our daughter and moved to Belgium. I only have seen my daughter once.

"So, I quit my job as a professor and headed to South America to see where life would take me."

Day 4 of 3

We woke up to everything white. A heavy snowfall covered the ground, the mountains, our tents, everything.

Behind us was a long ridge. Over breakfast, we discussed which pass we wanted to shoot for. By the time we made our decision, tore down camp, and packed up, the snow had melted, and a bright new day was upon us.

Me behind my snow-laden tent.

The climb up to the pass was steeper than the scree-covered mountain we had overcome in search of Lago Azul. The descent on the backside was steeper yet, but we were going down and the slipping scree sped up the descent. And just like that, we reached vegetation and warmer temperatures.

There was just one more short climb over a lush green, tree-less mountain. At the top, we were exposed to the intense wind Patagonia was known for. Every once in a while, a gust would hit us so hard it would cause us to stumble.

Wind was to Patagonia as haggis was to Scotland or vodka was to Russia. Trees grew bent or sideways here from the unrelenting wind. Most of the year, winds blew around twelve mph consistently. When the wind really picked up in the summer, seventy mph was not unheard of, and one hundred mph winds had been recorded. This was the play-ground of the eight wind gods I met head on in South Dakota.[43]

Barrow Island, off Australia, held the distinction of the highest ever recorded wind: 253 mph on April 10, 1996.

Descending, I came across a pile of garbage that some previous hiker left behind. Tucked away under a bush was a bunch of food pack-ages, some paper trash, an empty tube of toothpaste, plastic bags, and a wool sweater. Irritated, I shoved the trash in my pack and descended the backside of the mountain toward a greener and warmer setting.

Our last night, we built a fire, using some of the trash I collected as kindling. It was at this point we realized a campfire was what was missing the past few nights.

We had a great night, drinking the last liter of wine and sharing stories. Tomorrow we would be able to shower and enjoy a warm bed.

It should be noted: to build a campfire this far south in Patagonia was more of an exercise of creating a tremendous amount of smoke with the occasional flame. Everything was so wet and

43 TBATB

moist that even the dried out dead wood was saturated with water. So in retrospect, I suppose we built a camp-smoldering that night.

I take pride in my ability to start a campfire out in the wild, so it was humbling to not actually get a fire going. I later learned the indigenous Yaghan people of the area had the same problem. Their solution was simple, once they got their fires going, they kept them going, constantly, even carrying them if they had to. Spanish explorers passing through the channels would see fires dotting the shorelines and thus named the region Tierra del Fuego (Land of Fire).

Day 5 of 3

Something about returning from a multi-day trek puts a smile on your face. Even though this was day five of our three-day excursion, I wouldn't have changed anything about it.

I didn't care how long Hans needed to start his day. After eight hours, we reached the peat moss that we navigated through on day one. The trail we were on was a hard-packed dirt line that skirted the moss and dumped us out onto Ruta 3.

It wasn't long before we hitched a ride back with a guy who ended up inviting us to his cabin for dinner.

"Hey Cory, you want to go for a three-day trek?" Hans asked with a smile.

We partook in some of Hans's hash, enjoyed a pasta dinner, and chased it all down with wine.

I thought about our excursion.

Two guys from opposite sides of the world, having almost nothing in common, taking part in a rather challenging trek that could have ended up fatal as neither of us knew the other's experience level or capabilities.

Yet we managed to come together and work through and problem solve the challenges thrown at us. Negotiating which pass or valley to advance to and over. Navigating bogs and thickly vegetated forests, scree fields, and blizzards, and in the end, laughing and appreciating the time we had together, albeit they were just five days.

I was fried. Time to rest and have a drink.

Hans left two days later. I kept in touch with him for a while. Last report was he got a job with the Bolivian government as a hydrologist. I don't know if he was ever able to see his daughter again.

Oh, and the wool sweater I found. After having it laundered, it fit just fine, becoming a welcome addition to my wardrobe.

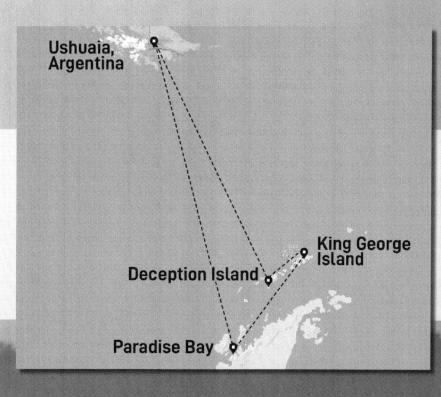

ANTARCTICA

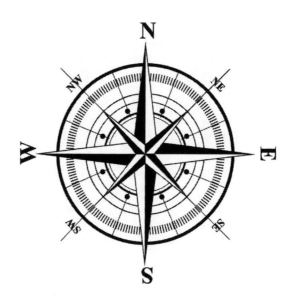

ANTARCTICA

"Opposite to the Arctic"

Day 1

Displacing 6600 tons and 364' long, we boarded the *RV Akademik Ioffe*, a Russian research vessel, which was hired to take us to Antarctica.

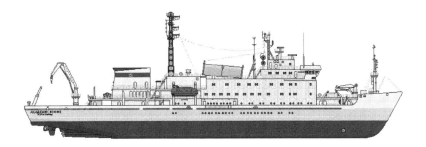

My cabin assignment was on Deck 4. My roommate was an Israeli guy by the name of Rory. Our names caused confusion when introducing ourselves to the other runners, who were under the impression we were traveling together. Neither of us having been with the group in Buenos Aires.

Rory made the same arrangement I did with the race director, which was to jump on the ship in Ushuaia. He had no intention of running the marathon.

When you're backpacking around, meeting people in hostels or on buses, you heard about so many things to do and opportunities that were out there that were not written in any guidebook. One of the rumors was that if you kept your ear to the ground,[44] you might be able to jump on a ship or sailboat headed to Antarctica. That was how Rory found himself here.

Deck 3 was sort of the main deck. This was where the dining room, bar, and small lounge were all located. The back was an observation deck where a couple of Zodiacs were stored along with a crane to load and unload equipment.

Deck 4, where our cabin was, also had the Forward Observation Deck and rescue boats hung from the railings at this level.

Deck 5 had more cabins and the infirmary.

Deck 6 was the bridge, radio, and chartroom. The bridge was always available to enter and offered a fantastic view.

It was smooth sailing as we moved east through the Beagle Channel, which served to separate Argentina and Chile starting just west of Ushuaia. This border designation meant that the most southern islands of South America belonged to Chile, not Argentina. There had been many border disputes between the two countries over the years.

---

44 Another US Americanism that originated in the 1800s, literally means to put your ear to the ground to hear horses or footsteps.

We passed Puerto Williams, Chile, to the south. It was now a hamlet, but decades later, Chile would upgrade it to a city, stealing away the title of "World's Southernmost City" from Argentina. And the battle played on.

The remains of the *MV Logos* shipwreck sat rusting on an outcrop of rocks toward the mouth of the channel.

The ship passed along Isla Picton, Isla Lennox, Isla Nueva, and finally, the famous Cabo de Hornos—Cape Horn.

Our next stop was Deception Island, 625 miles away.

My book of choice for this journey was *Endurance: Shackleton's Incredible Voyage* by Alfred Lansing.

There were a total of eighty-five of us from around the world. I sat reading my book in the lounge. A woman in her fifties sat down next to me.

"I don't recall seeing you in Buenos Aires," she said.

"Yes, that is true. I was in Ushuaia already."

"Why were you there alone?"

"I've been working my way down by land and worked out a deal with the marathon director to jump on with you guys in Ushuaia."

"Really, where did you start?"

"I started by bicycle in Minneapolis, Minnesota, biking to California. Left my bike in Carmel at my cousin's and made my way down by land. Sort of making it up as I go."

"Really! My husband and I are from Minneapolis, Minnesota. How long have you been traveling?"

"Hmmm. I left late August 2001," I paused to do the math on my fingers, "seven months." I showed her my seven fingers like a kid did when they told you how old they were.

"Seven months! Wow, that sounds fantastic. Are you from Minneapolis?"

"Minneapolis was my last home. So, do you know a guy by the name of Mark Brunsvold?"

In Minneapolis, the marathon running community was sort of a close-knit clan. At least, it felt that way in the 1990s when I started running marathons. Mark is a local legend, known for running marathons while pushing his daughter Amanda, who was in a wheelchair due to her cerebral palsy, along with him.

"Mark, did Amanda beat you again?" I would ask him.

"Yep, she always finishes a second ahead of me."

Mark and Amanda were the Dick and Rick Hoyt of Minneapolis. I didn't know Mark really well at the time, but he was one of my Uncle Steve's best friends.

"Yes, I know Mark."

"How do you know him?" she asked.

"Well, I really don't know him well, but he is a good friend of my uncle."

"What is your uncle's name?"

"Steve."

She paused. "Steve Heckenlaible?"

You can well imagine how shocked I was that she blurted out my uncle's name and pronounced the last name correctly.

I stared at her for a moment then responded, "Uh, yeah. Steve Heckenlaible, that's my uncle. Do you know him?"

"Mark is my brother. I've known Steve very well for decades. As a matter of fact, I know your Aunt Mary, your Uncle Charlie, and Helen."

"Helen! You know my Grandma Helen!?"

"My name is Chris. My husband Conrad and I own Hoigaard's."[45]

"You own Hoigaard's? Well, small world. My name is Cory."

Here I was, heading to the bottom of the world, on a Russian ship with eighty-five people from all over the world, and one of them knew my grandma.

She questioned me for an hour about my trip and the details of what I had seen and done. At dinner, she introduced me to her husband. He wasn't as interested in my trip as she was.

I watched the sunset on the back deck along with a few others and then read a little from my book *Endurance: Shackleton's Incredible Voyage*.

Later that night, I couldn't sleep and found myself wandering around the ship. I ran into one of the Russian crew members who was, more or less, out of sight during most of the trip. Their jobs were not customer-facing. The Russian and I talked briefly, and he invited me to a lower deck.

The Russian crew were singing, dancing, and more than willing to share with me some of their vodka and fresh-caught crabs. You don't sip vodka with Russians; you shoot it. You shoot it frequently

---

45 Hoigaard's was a local outdoor outfitter in Minneapolis, Minnesota, with a focus on winter sports.

and with purpose and then you celebrate life with more dancing and more singing and more vodka.

By the end of the night, I stumbled up to my cabin with a firm grasp of the Russian language. Well, at least, a tiny grasp. I was able to say the following:

Privet	Hello
Spasibo	Thank you
Do svidaniya	Goodbye
Zatknis' i potseluy menya	Shut up and kiss me

The last one I learned from the Russian female crew member who, late into the night, said to me "Zatknis' i potseluy menya."

I complied.

Day 2

One word—Epic.

At one point, the side exterior door to the dining room swung open, and it felt like a thousand gallons of water filled the room, drenching everything and everyone from floor to ceiling, head to toe.

If sea sickness was a concern, you might as well just say no to a trip to Antarctica. Those of us not affected by seasickness worked our way to the bridge to visually experience the massive waves tossing us around. The bow rose straight up and then straight down. Waves twenty-feet-high exploded over the bow with winds forty mph as we moved south, deeper through the Drake Passage.

At an average depth of 12,500' where the Pacific and Atlantic meet and with no land obstructions anywhere at that latitude, the volume of water that surged through the passage every second was equal to five thousand Amazon Rivers.

"THIS, THEN, WAS THE DRAKE PASSAGE, THE
MOST DREADED BIT OF OCEAN ON THE GLOBE—
AND RIGHTLY SO. HERE NATURE HAS BEEN GIVEN
A PROVING GROUND ON WHICH TO DEMONSTRATE
WHAT SHE CAN DO IF LEFT ALONE. THE RESULTS ARE
IMPRESSIVE."
– Ernest Shackleton

We were getting our money's worth this day, and I was so happy we hit these fierce and outrageous waters.

Once back to calmer waters, one of the crew members told us that roughly twenty thousand sailors and eight hundred ships had sunk making this crossing. Prudent that he waited to share this information.

I found a seat in the lounge and continued my book until dinner. We would see land come sunrise.

Day 3

As we approached King George Island, I looked east hoping to catch a glimpse of Elephant Island. It was over one hundred miles away, and my hope was thwarted.

I had just been reading about how Shackleton and his men had been stranded on Elephant Island for four months before finally being rescued. Shackleton, along with five others, managed to sail the twenty-two-foot lifeboat, *James Caird*, eight hundred miles through the Southern Ocean and make it to South Georgia Island thanks to the navigational precision of Frank Worsley.

The entire story was utterly fantastic.

Our first stop was Deception Island.

While appearing like an island, it was in fact a caldera of an active volcano, hence the name Deception Island. The captain steered the ship into the caldera known as Whalers Bay. During the whaling station's height, it was said that you could almost walk across the entire bay on the carcasses of whales being harvested. That bit was shared with us by our guide.

The process of unloading the Zodiacs was impressive. Before we had time to get our life jackets on, the first Zodiac was waiting at the bottom of the staircase that led from Deck 3 to the ocean. The first group was taken to shore. I took the third boat.

Being that Deception Island was still an active volcano, our guide handed a couple of us a shovel and told us to dig a hole, not deep, but about fifteen feet in diameter. Rory and I dug a hole. It immediately filled with water.

"Get in."

"What?"

"Take off your clothes and get in."

We stripped down to our underwear and laid in the hole. The water was heated by the volcano to a pleasant ninety degrees. When the water cooled down, you just dug a little with your hands and it was warm again.

The world is a pretty amazing place.

Enjoying volcano-heated pool on Deception Island.

Day 4

The big day. This would be my ninth marathon.

I started running marathons in 1998. A friend who I hadn't seen in a while called me out of the blue for lunch. It was July 1998. I met her, and she looked radiant. I mean she glowed. Her skin looked healthy, and she had a nice tan.

"My goodness, Shari, you look amazing! What have you been doing?"

"Well, I wanted to tell you that I started running marathons and thought of you. I run with a group and they are really fun, and I wonder if you'd like to join."

"Running? Ha ha. Umm no. I really don't like running."

"When did you last run?"

"I don't know, from the cops in college."

"Look, the Twin Cities Marathon registration closes today. Sign up and then sign up with my running group. It will be a lot of fun. Plus, there are more women than men. Single women."

The marathon office was three blocks from where I worked downtown, and I decided to "run" over there to sign up. After a block, I was wiped out. There was no way I could run a marathon. I couldn't even run a block.

November 4, 1998, I completed the Twin Cities Marathon, had a new group of friends, and a different perspective on life.

In 1999, I ran Chicago, Mardi Gras, Grandma's, Disney, and Honolulu.

In 2000, it was Long Beach and Vermont City.

The Antarctica Marathon was to take place on King George Island. That morning the ocean was pretty choppy and there was talk about not going ashore.

The year before, 2001, the participants of the Antarctica Marathon had the same situation. Instead of actually going ashore, they ran the whole marathon on the ship: 26.2 miles on a 364-foot-long ship. That was about 380 laps.

We were all willing to risk the big waves and take the Zodiacs to the shore of King George Island.

By the time we landed, we were all drenched. Not the best way to start a marathon, but the Russians at Bellingshausen research station let us come in, dry off as much as we could, and warm up while the Zodiacs brought more of the runners and the race coordinators got organized.

During the marathon, we were told the wind got up to around fifty miles per hour. Snow blew sideways as we ran along the frozen mud roads that would lead us out and back to the Uruguayan Artigas Base then back to Bellingshausen and on to the Chilean Base Presidente Eduardo Frei Montalva and then south to the Chinese Great Wall Station.

The winner finished in four hours ten minutes. I finished thirty-three out of eighty-five in five hours thirty-nine minutes.

After we returned to the ship, the race director, who had all our passports securely placed in a safe on the ship, had our passports stamped at the Russian Bellingshausen base, one of my favorite passport stamps to date.

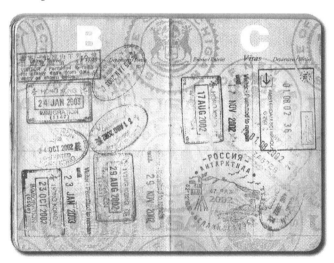

My passport with stamp of Russian Antarctica base.

That night after dinner, we watched a slideshow from the days' events and all shared our own story of how our day went, celebrating with cocktails at the bar. A few of us went to the observation deck to watch the incredible Antarctic sunset. The waters were free from waves as the RV *Akademik Ioffe* made its way south.

Days 5 and 6

The captain let us know when we crossed into the Antarctic Circle, one of the five latitudes used to divide maps at 66°33'S.

I didn't even know this was on the agenda. If you were to ask me if I would have found myself in the Antarctic Circle, I would have smiled and replied, "Yeah right." Never did I think I would be in Antarctica. To add a cherry on top of this, we were given the option to camp on the peninsula. On the actual continent of Antarctica. I was the first off the ship. Ten of us camped. I had my own tent and went solo.

Enjoying the sunset in Antarctica.

We explored Paradise Bay with its smattering of small icebergs. The water was trying to decide whether or not it wanted to freeze. The Zodiacs allowed us to examine the glaciers' intense blue million-year-old ice.

At the Lemaire Channel, humpback whales joined us, perhaps curious. Then they started to breach.

"Do you see the tails of the humpbacks?" Our guide pointed as one of the whales slapped its tail.

"Yes," the ten of us in the Zodiac said simultaneously.

"The tail on the humpback is like a fingerprint. They all have their own unique markings."

The whales continued to give us an impressive show.

This trip to Antarctica just kept getting better and better. After our night camping, a few minke whales escorted us north for a while and then disappeared. I sat on the back observation deck while the sun set on my last glance of Antarctica.

In two days, I would be back in Ushuaia. One more night at Sabastian's and then back to the United States.

Last day in Ushuaia with Sabastian (the guy, not the dog).

My last morning, I walked to the airport. I could have taken a taxi but decided to take in the last of my surroundings. It was all magical and foreign, yet everywhere I had been was comfortable and felt like home.

Seven months ago, I clipped my foot into a pedal and left home on a two-month leave of absence. It seemed like a lifetime ago.

AFTERWORD

You may have experienced this. If not, you may have heard that when someone comes back from an extended trip like this, the first thing they struggle with is all the decisions. For example, just think about grabbing a Coke. There is: Coke, Diet Coke, Diet Cherry Coke, Coke Zero, Vanilla Coke... you get the idea. Don't get me started on the wall of toothpaste one can choose from.

It was a little overwhelming at first, but I quickly acclimated back to US American society. My first meal at the Houston Airport? A footlong Spicy Italian Subway sandwich with extra mayo.[46]

Back in Phoenix, I acquired a 1974 VW Bus. Red with a white roof. Inside was an incredibly comfortable bed. The storage offered more room than the possessions I carried in my pack. There was also a sink, fridge, table, and AM/FM radio.

Driving west to San Diego, I headed up the Pacific Coast Highway to Carmel and picked up my bike that I had left at cousin Becky's.[47]

Just past Santa Barbara, I picked up a hitchhiker. A little karmic return of the ride received from Gen and David.

He was about my age and had a really nice backpack, so I figured what the heck. It wasn't long before he shared with me that he was headed to Alaska to work on a fishing boat. It wasn't long after that, I realized he was a total dick and had some major anger issues. Every question I asked, he responded with violent yelling.

"So, do you have any tattoos?" I asked.

"No, man! No distinguishing marks for the cops!"

And so, I didn't ask any more questions and couldn't wait to drop him off in Carmel.

It was springtime. I retraced some of the route that I had biked to California. Sort of amazed at some of the long desolate stretches of road and steep ascents. Occasionally, I stopped, got out of the bus, and stood alongside the road looking at that impossible-to-catch vanishing point and asked myself, "Did I really ride this on my bicycle?"

It was the first week of April when I pulled into my driveway.

I had my future wife waiting for me in London, so I immediately went to work getting the house ready to sell. Chop chop.

The housing market was scorching hot, and I sold the house before even putting it on the market. The transaction added a nice chunk of change to my bank account, which meant more freedom.

47 TBATB

May 20-30, I spent a week in Moab, Utah, mountain biking with some friends.

June 7, I stored the VW Bus and the rest of my personal belongings, which had been reduced to five plastic bins.

PART 2:
I KNEW WHERE I WAS GOING
THIS TIME...

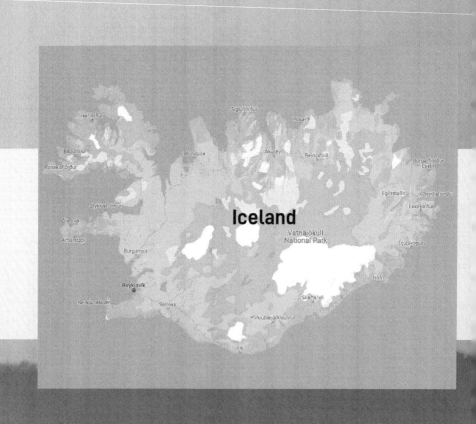

ICELAND: "LAND OF FIRE AND ICE"

Here, There
Hither and Yon
This Way or That Way

ICELAND

"Land of Fire and Ice"

J une 8, 2002, I departed for Iceland.

TO BE CONTINUED...

"I MAY NOT HAVE GONE WHERE I INTENDED TO GO,
BUT I THINK I HAVE ENDED UP WHERE I INTENDED
TO BE."

– Douglas Adams

ABOUT THE AUTHOR

Cory Mortensen has ridden his collection of bicycles over a million miles of asphalt, dirt, mud, and backroads. In addition to the cross-country journey detailed in his previous book, *The Buddha and the Bee*, he has traveled to over fifty-five countries, cycled from Minneapolis to Colorado solo to raise money for children born with congenital heart defects. He's completed sixteen marathons on five continents, and survived three days of running with the bulls in Spain.

Cory is a certified Advanced PADI diver, and has enjoyed taking in life under the waves in locations all over the world. In 2003, he took time off from roaming, and accidentally started and built a company which he sold in 2013. That same year he married his best friend, and explored the state of Texas for two years. The couple sold everything they owned, jumped on a plane to Ecuador and volunteered, trekked, and explored South America for sixteen months before returning to Phoenix, Arizona, where he works as a consultant and bestselling author.

Contact the author at cory@corymortensen.com
www.thebuddhaandthebee.com
www.corymortensen.com
Follow Cory on Facebook and Instagram.

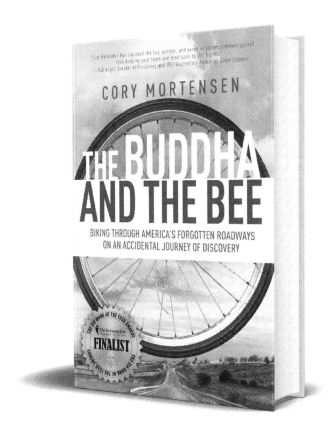

The Buddha and the Bee is Cory Mortensen's first memoir. He shares how a two-month leave of absence redefined his life's trajectory of sitting behind a desk and his decision to break society's chains so he could live life on his terms.

Find Cory's books at www.TheBuddhaAndTheBee.com
Available in paperback, hardcover with color photos, and ebook.

Made in the USA
Middletown, DE
10 November 2022

14571417R00189